THE LAST STAND

A Journey Through the Ancient Cliff-Face
Forest of the Niagara Escarpment

Peter E. Kelly & Douglas W. Larson

Foreword by Sarah Harmer

NATURAL HERITAGE BOOKS
A MEMBER OF THE DUNDURN GROUP
TORONTO

Published by Natural Heritage Books
A Member of The Dundurn Group
3 Church Street, Suite 500
Toronto, Ontario, M5E 1M2, Canada
www.dundurn.com

Library and Archives Canada Cataloguing in Publication

Kelly, Peter E., 1963-
    The last stand : a journey through the ancient cliff-face forest of the Niagara Escarpment / Peter E. Kelly & Douglas W. Larson ; foreword by Sarah Harmer.

Includes bibliographical references and index.
ISBN 978-1-897045-19-0

    1. Thuja occidentalis—Niagara Escarpment. 2. Thuja occidentalis—Ontario. 3. Cliff ecology—Niagara Escarpment. 4. Old-growth forests—Niagara Escarpment. 5. Forest ecology—Niagara Escarpment. 6. Niagara Escarpment. I. Larson, Douglas W. (Douglas William), 1949- II. Title.

QH106.2.O5K44 2007   585'.4   C2006-906051-7

    1   2   3   4   5   11   10   09   08   07

All photographs and b&w sketches are by Peter Kelly unless otherwise indicated.
Front cover: A vulture soars above the cliffs at Smokey Head, on the eastern shore of the Bruce Peninsula. Back cover: A view of Hamilton from the Escarpment.

Cover and text design by Sari Naworynski
Edited by Jane Gibson
Printed and bound in Canada by Friesens
Printed on Garda Art Silk

We acknowledge the support of the Canada Council for the Arts and the Ontario Arts Council for our publishing program. We also acknowledge the financial support of the Government of Canada through the Book Publishing Industry Development Program and The Association for the Export of Canadian Books and the Government of Canada through the Ontario Book Publishers Tax Credit Program and the Ontario Media Development Corporation.

For Dad and David who always supported what I've done, even if it meant hanging off cliffs for months on end (PK), and for Nick, Nathan, and Gin – may you learn from the trees and grow old slowly (DWL).

TABLE OF CONTENTS

ACKNOWLEDGEMENTS

We would like to gratefully acknowledge the following agencies who provided support for our research on the eastern white cedar forests of the Niagara Escarpment over the years: the Bruce Trail Association, the Coalition on the Niagara Escarpment (CONE), the EJLB Foundation, the Escarpment Biosphere Conservancy, Global Forest, the McLean Foundation, the Natural Sciences and Engineering Research Council of Canada, the Nature Conservancy of Canada, the Ontario Heritage Foundation, the Ontario Ministry of the Environment, Ontario Parks, Parks Canada, The Richard Ivey Foundation and Swish Maintenance Ltd. We would particularly like to thank Reese Halter from Global Forest for his enthusiasm and encouragement for both our research and the book, and Marvi Ricker and The Richard Ivey Foundation who gave us the funds to get the Niagara Escarpment Ancient Tree Atlas Project off the ground. Both sponsors stepped up at a time when financial support for ecological research in Ontario had evaporated. We would also like to thank the landowners who have graciously allowed us access to the Niagara Escarpment cliff faces that cross their properties, namely Sandy Stuart, Jeff and Nancy Bettridge, Margaret Dodgson, Parks Canada, Ontario Parks, Ministry of Natural Resources, Niagara Peninsula Conservation Authority, Niagara Parks Commission, Brock University, City of St. Catharines, Bruce Trail Association, Hamilton Region Conservation Authority, Royal Botanical Gardens, Halton Region Conservation Authority, Milton Limestone and Grey Sauble Conservation Authority. If we couldn't have access to the cliffs, we could never have made our discoveries and we definitely could not have put this book together.

Many of the historical photos and references were located with the help of staff at various archives and libraries. These would include Shannon McFadyen at the Niagara Escarpment Commission, Elysia

DeLaurentis at the Wellington County Museum and Archives, Linda Twitchell at the Halton Region Museum and Archives and Ann-Marie Collins at the Bruce County Museum and Archives. The Metropolitan Toronto Reference Library, Burlington Public Library, Grey County Archives and the Archives of Ontario were also valuable sources of both photos and information.

FOREWORD
by Sarah Harmer

Find yourself alone in calm woods, leaves drifting to forest floor, creeks running downhill under fallen tree bridges, and leave your footprints in the mud. Let yourself be inspired by a place that continues to breathe after you leave. Up here on the Niagara Escarpment systems are ancient. Water springs from the cavernous rock and forests grow old. Ponds are full of memory and team with fish, frogs and spotted newts. Hawks and owls, herons and salamanders all find their niche among the wetlands and woods, and through fertile fields coyote and deer secure food and safe passage.

This is where I grew up. An outcrop of the Niagara Escarpment in Burlington, Ontario. A place called Mount Nemo. The cliffs of Mount Nemo hold some of North America's oldest living trees and over the centuries countless humans have gazed from its sheer heights across rich panoramas.

Imagine the past in this place, pullovers of Time layered in familiar yarns and colours. Four hundred years ago, in the early 1600s the Native Peoples who lived atop Mount Nemo were called the Attawandaron. Their lack of involvement in the fur-trading wars between neighbouring Huron and Iroquois tribes led the French explorers to call them Les Neutral. The Attawandaron (Neutral) First Nation lived on Mount Nemo in longhouses that were organized by the female family line, grew corn, beans and squash, and valued the fruits of the butternut and walnut trees. They were not accomplished on the water and so chose high places to establish settlements so they could look out across Lake Ontario in search of approaching canoes. In 35 years of living here my family and I had never heard of these Native people, let alone known that they'd once lived in the backfields. Delving further we learned of Jikonsaseh, the Neutral Peace Queen who travelled with Hiawatha, spreading the word of the Peace Maker and working to establish peace between warring nations.

I learned about this 400-year-old Attawandaron (Neutral) settlement through an archaeological dig that was undertaken as part of a recent quarry application that proposes to rezone roughly two hundred acres atop Mount Nemo from Escarpment Rural Land to Mineral Extraction Land for a below-water-table extraction operation.

In this glorious book, as they describe the geology and formation of the Niagara Escarpment, authors Peter Kelly and Doug Larson write, "In the short term the Niagara Escarpment isn't going anywhere." Unfortunately, huge amounts of the Escarpment are getting hauled away, five days a week, from sun-up to sundown. Gravel trucks climb to the top of the escarpment brow and descend with full loads of ancient seabed limestone crushed into gravel. The ancient ecosystems on top on this rock and the rock itself are removed forever.

Allow yourself to be inspired by this book, by these resilient and remarkable ancient forests, by the cultural and natural history that lays the foundation for our lives today. Let the Niagara Escarpment breathe and let yourself breathe. In that breath find the inspiration and the passion to speak for this land and its irreplaceable wonder.

SARAH HARMER

PREFACE
The Two Trees

Two trees, amid those leafy shade
The warbling birds their vigils paid,
Stood neighbours – each as noble tree
In height and girth as one might see.
The one, sequestered in the vale,
All sheltered from the boisterous gale,
Had passed his days in soft repose;
The other from the cliff arose,
And bore the brunt of stormy wind
That lashed him oft in frenzy blind.

A day there happed when from the north
Aquilon drave his forces forth,
And hurled them headlong on the rock
Where, proudly poised to meet the shock,
Our bold tree stood. In gallant might,
He took the gage of proffered fight,
And though in every fibre wrung,
Kept every fibre still upstrung.

"Thou tremblest!" cried the sheltered tree,
"Thine own the folly! Come to me.
Here no wild tempest rocks our boughs-
Scarce may it bend our haughty brows-
Scarce may a breeze our branches kiss-
From every harm a shelter this."

No word replied the storm-tried tree,
But, wrestling for the mastery,
He bowed and straightened, writhed and shook,
And firmer of the rock he took
A tightening clutch with grip of steel,
Nor once the storm-fiend made him reel;
And when his weary foe passed by,
Still towered he proudly to the sky.

Then through the vale the winged blast
For the first time in fury passed,
As through ripe grain the sickles go,
Widespread he scattered fear and woe;
Prone fell the tree–so safe before
'Mid ruin dire, to rise no more.

He cannot fall who knows to fight
With stern adversity aright.
But soon is laid the victim low,
That knows not how to ward a blow.[1]

SARAH ANNE CURZON, 1887

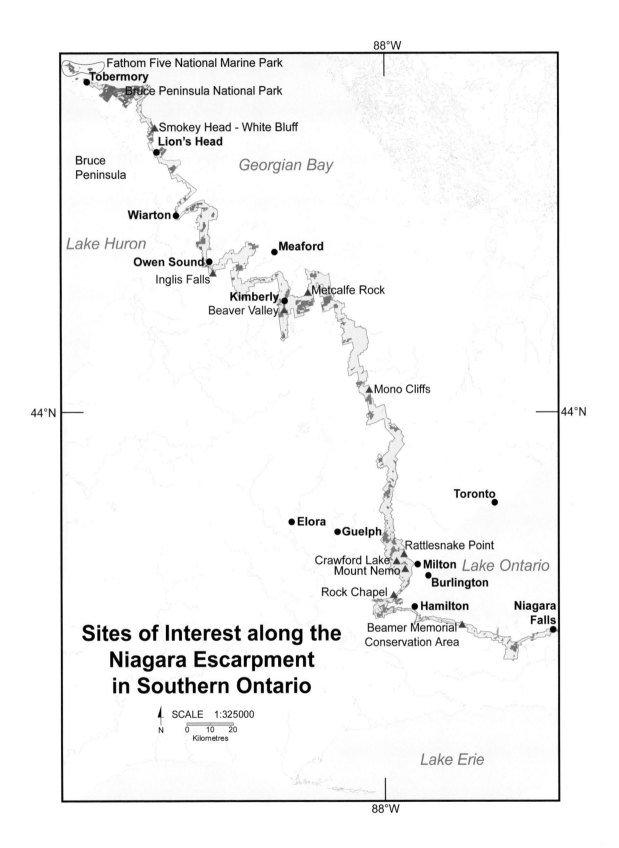

Fathom Five National Marine Park
Tobermory
Bruce Peninsula National Park

▲ Smokey Head - White Bluff
Lion's Head

Bruce
Peninsula

Georgian Bay

Lake Huron

Wiarton●

●**Meaford**

Owen Sound●
▲ Inglis Falls

Kimberly● ▲ Metcalfe Rock
Beaver Valley ▲

▲ Mono Cliffs

44°N

●Toronto

●**Elora**
●**Guelph**

Rattlesnake Point
Crawford Lake ▲ ●**Milton** *Lake Ontario*
Mount Nemo ▲
●**Burlington**
Rock Chapel ▲
●**Hamilton** **Niagara Falls**
Beamer Memorial ▲
Conservation Area ●

44°N

Sites of Interest along the
Niagara Escarpment
in Southern Ontario

SCALE 1:325000
N
0 10 20
Kilometres

Lake Erie

INTRODUCTION

Old trees are not necessarily big. We know you find that hard to believe, but we don't blame you. Our whole lives we have been fed with images of stately and majestic stands of old-growth forests; living cathedrals that tower above the landscape. Trees so massive that a dozen people joined hand-in-hand could barely encircle one. Most of us can recall having seen a grainy black and white image of an old car driving through the centre of a California redwood tree. We're not sure where or when we saw it, or where the tree actually grows, but it has made one lasting impression on us; that is a very big – and a very old – tree.

Indeed, big trees *are* impressive. They teach humility. They are a testament to the persistence of nature. That tree started out as one of millions of seeds scattered on the forest floor. Now look at it! For the most part, at least within the same species, big trees are also very old. In most level-ground habitats, there is a strong association between a tree's diameter and its age. It makes sense; we've all watched trees in our yards or our communities grow to significant heights over the course of our lives.

This "upside-down" cedar is only 2.5 metres "tall" but is over 350 years old.

1

But sometimes size is deceiving. A local Guelph resident once had us visit her recently collapsed sugar maple tree that was 2.6 metres in diameter. She was certain that it was a forest ancient that had been spared the lumberman's axe. Close inspection of the massive tree, however, showed annual tree rings almost two centimetres across and an age less than 100 years. It turned out that the tree had grown in the location of an old chicken coop!

Along the cliff faces of the Niagara Escarpment in southern Ontario, Canada, there is a remarkable forest that defies the standard paradigm that old is big. Here, centuries-old eastern white cedars cling to the hollows, ledges and cracks that cut across the face. These trees are the antithesis of our standard perceptions of old-growth. Most of the trees would fit comfortably in a living room. The oldest trees are less than seven metres "tall" (we'll get to this), many considerably less. In an environment where gravity is a prominent ecological force, "tall" or "height" are not adequate descriptors. "Length" is probably more accurate, for the axes of these trees can travel in any direction when they emerge from the cliff. In some cases, the tree is rooted on the face *above* its crown, a situation that could never be duplicated on level ground!

It's not just their size that makes these trees remarkable. Their unusual morphologies reflect the hardships that they have endured over centuries. While we cannot yet reconstruct the events that affected any one tree, we do know that each old tree has been shaped by dozens of traumatic events over the course of its life. Just like the cliff tree in Sarah Curzon's story of "The Two Trees," they bear battle scars from ice storms, gales, heavy snowfalls, falling rocks, small

Towering giant sequoia forests of California satisfy many people's perceptions of stereotypical old-growth forest. While these Sequoias may be several magnitudes larger, they are not necessarily older than cliff-face cedars.

Only a narrow strip of bark keeps this 540-year-old cedar from succumbing to the elements.

mammals and the perpetual pull of gravity. As any given cedar seed fluttered through the air and landed within the rocky confines of the cliff face, it came to rest in a spot that would control the amount of light, heat and moisture available to it. After it germinated and survived to adulthood, the tree's morphology eventually recorded the environmental conditions that occurred at that spot for centuries.

While no two escarpment trees look alike, they share distinguishing features. For one, many of the oldest trees appear dead. At first glance, their most notable and eye-catching feature is an abundance of bleached, barkless, dead wood. Often the original axis is dead but remains attached to the tree, projecting into space like the prow of a ship or a sail-less mast. Whitened tentacle-like dead branches hang downwards giving the tree an otherworldly appearance. New growth advances over the stumps of broken or dead branches. Living branches stretch outwards for light. Roots weave their way along fissures or ledges. They seek out cavities on the face and plunge into networks of small cracks and fissures. Sometimes

A 500-year-old cedar greets the rising sun on a cliff face near Milton.

The dead tip of this living 507-year-old cedar reaches out to the waters of Georgian Bay.

there is soil; sometimes there is not. The trees become contorted and twisted with age, living barber poles where strips of barked wood spiral around parallel strips of barkless dead wood. The cedar's trunk develops a sharp taper with advancing age and the base becomes increasingly gnarled. If Yoda were a tree, he might look like one of these.

Despite their appearance, the cedars are actually flourishing in a vertical environment so harsh that only robust and colourful lichens and a few species of hardy flowering plants can grow. It is hardly the environment anyone would explore if the goal were to find old-growth forest. Their discovery by us was more of a fortuitous accident than anything else. They may still have been unknown if our research group hadn't bothered to investigate the seemingly unrelated topic of hiking impacts on the cliff-edge forest. Cliffs are the main reason these trees have persevered, but they are also the same reason they went undiscovered for so long.

Cliffs select against human intrusion. While the rest of southern Ontario's woodlands were being converted into lumber and arable land, the cliffs of the Niagara Escarpment were ignored because they couldn't be accessed or farmed and the stunted trees (if they were noticed at all!) simply weren't worth the effort of harvesting. By 1978, only 0.07% of southern Ontario's land base supported forest stands with trees older than 120 years. Considering that white cedars up to 1,320 years in age have survived in a landscape completely altered from its natural state of being, it's hard to believe that there hasn't been a more concerted effort to place this forest under some level of protection.

The answer lies in the habitat in which they grow. To a casual observer, the trees are difficult to appreciate. Everyone who travels to Sequoia National Park in California can saunter to or wheel themselves up to the General Sherman tree, a 2,100-year-old giant sequoia that is the largest tree on earth. The ancient cedars are more elusive. Unless you're a rock climber, it is difficult to get a good look at one of these old trees. The talus at the base of most cliffs is a jumble of ankle-twisting rocks, poison ivy and unruly plants. Viewing the cliff face from the cliff edge is difficult and unsafe. Make no mistake about it, this is certainly a good thing for the trees' sake, but it also means that they remain outside the public's collective consciousness. It is more difficult to appreciate and thus protect something if it remains invisible to the public eye. Our inherent bias towards bigger being better is a growing hurdle that is difficult to overcome. In a world where shiny SUVs and Monster Trucks are king, it's difficult to find fans of the durable albeit ugly 1984 Chevette. They aren't the SUVs of the botanical world, but the ancient cedars have a timeless beauty in their stunted trunks and misshapen limbs.

The idea for this book sprang out conversations with Reese Halter of the Global Forest Society, a private foundation that co-sponsored a project that we started in 1998 called the Niagara Escarpment Ancient Tree Atlas Project. The principal goals of the Niagara Escarpment Ancient Tree Atlas Project were 1) to determine the age and location of the oldest trees at individual Escarpment sites, 2) to determine the habitat variables that lead to longevity in this species and 3) to increase public awareness of the ancient cedars. Part of the data collection involved photographing individual trees or sketching them when the cliff face or other trees thwart efforts to obtain an unobstructed photograph. These photographs and sketches were included in three reports that were sent to the landowners and land managers of the surveyed properties. Reese felt that the third objective could most easily be satisfied by the preparation of a book on the trees and we agreed.

We have made every effort to present to you the complete story of the eastern white cedar or the arbor vitae. This includes information not just on the ancient cedars that cling to the Niagara Escarpment cliffs but also on the historical importance of white cedar to both our Native cultures and eastern Canada's earliest settlers. It is often difficult to distinguish historical references to "cedar" between eastern white cedar and eastern red cedar *Juniperus virginiana*. While their natural ranges are relatively distinct (white cedar occupies the northern half of eastern North America and red cedar the southern half), there is some overlap in the northern American States and southern Ontario. While eastern red cedar was similarly important to other First Nations' groups, we have avoided references to it because it is the arbor vitae that comprise the ancient forests of the Niagara Escarpment.

We look at this book as a conservation effort. Since their "discovery" in 1988, there have been minimal efforts on the part of landowners or governing bodies to implement strategies directly aimed at protecting this ancient forest, even though it has proven to be the most ancient and, until recently, least disturbed forest stand in eastern North America, hence the title of the book. We believe that part of the problem is that many people still do not have a good idea of what these ancient cedars look like. Permanent protection will be impossible if the status quo is maintained. This book will provide you with a comprehensive look at a forest that is a unique and special part of North America's natural heritage. It is hoped that through it, you will develop an appreciation for both the Niagara Escarpment and the ancient cedars that call it home. They have captured our imagination for almost eighteen years. We hope they do the same for you.

CHAPTER 1

THE NIAGARA ESCARPMENT

Ontario: a province, a lake, a county. Properly it should be On-tar-ack or On-da-rack. On means "high," tarack, "rocks"; that is, "rocks standing high in or near the water." The reference is probably to the Niagara Escarpment.[1]
William F. Moore, 1930

Rattlesnake Point rises above the fields of Halton Region.

To the casual observer, southern Ontario is boring and flat. The fact that this "flatness" is actually a complex mosaic of hills and valleys is of little consequence to most people (outside the cycling community!). The truth is that these hills and valleys have never inspired the same passion among writers and artists as, for example, the Rocky Mountains or the Appalachians, both impressive on a massive scale. These geological masterpieces demand attention and command respect. They have transcended the relative boredom of their surrounding landscapes and we, too, are impressed with them. Southern Ontario, on the other hand, has been little more than a dumping ground for massive glaciers that intermittently ploughed their way across the northern half of the continent. When climate warmed, they shrank northwards. The glaciers weren't particularly neat about it, either. Think of a roadside after snowmelt in the spring. Debris churned up by scouring was dumped everywhere. The continental glaciers were undoubtedly an impressive sight (imagine an ice wall over a kilometre thick!), but the slurry they left behind, considerably less so.

As rivers and streams dissected the landscape and plants and animals recolonized the surface, southern Ontario developed its character. Many of the bumps and hollows that dot the landscape tell a fascinating story, but it is the Niagara Escarpment that is its showpiece – the showy orchid amongst the clover. Take your friends or family down one of many Escarpment back roads and watch how everybody strains for a view of the cliff face. It isn't surprising that a visual encounter with the Escarpment is treated with such fanfare. It is as if humans need rock – we like to see mountains, outcrops and cliffs. They comfort us. We appreciate their aesthetics even if we don't know why. If located elsewhere, the Niagara Escarpment might be overshadowed by more impressive topography, but here in southern Ontario it is a visual vertical refuge from the horizontal glacial landscape. It cuts its way from the Niagara Peninsula in the south to the Bruce Peninsula in the north, stretching onto the islands off Tobermory. From there it continues onto Manitoulin Island. Luckily, it provides a natural corridor for plant and animal life, while acting as a natural barrier to human traffic. Much of the land along the Escarpment is relatively undisturbed because it was such an obstacle to the expansion of Europeans in southern Ontario.

The real story of the Niagara Escarpment actually begins over 400 million years ago when North America looked very different than it does today. This was during the period in geological history known as the Silurian. An inland sea covered the interior of the continent during this time in an area now known as the Michigan Basin. Large numbers of dead marine invertebrates and sediments accumulated at the bottom of this sea. These sediments would eventually form the dolomitic caprock that we now see on the Niagara Escarpment. For 130 million years, the land remained underwater and layer upon layer of sediments and organisms accumulated on top of the Silurian deposits. The tremendous weight of these overlying layers exposed the underlying deposits to intense pressures that chemically transformed the sediment/invertebrate mix into rock.

If the Silurian dolomites mark the upper layers of the Escarpment cliff face, what happened to everything else deposited over the last 400 million years? In short, there is no way of knowing.

The Niagara Escarpment was formed from sediments and the bodies of invertebrates that accumulated at the bottom of a large inland sea nearly 400 million years ago.

Clearly, the rock and/or sediments that had accumulated here have eroded away. Much of this erosion likely occurred soon after the disappearance of the inland sea and the development of drainage basins on the emergent land. Surface water then removed the overlying sediment. Undoubtedly, some layers of sedimentary rocks did form after the Silurian, but they have now disappeared.

The Niagara Escarpment has probably existed as a landform for millions of years. Once the overlying deposits were removed, the dolomite and limestone resisted erosion more so than the underlying shale. It is likely that the Escarpment has been exposed as a series of rock outcrops or cliffs ever since. Versions of Ontario's Niagara Escarpment that predate the last glaciation formed several kilometres north and east of its present-day location. The cliffs of this early Escarpment were also considerably lower than the present-day cliffs because the caprock layers were thinner. Since the stratigraphic layers of rock dip south – to westward towards the centre of the Michigan Basin, the exposed rock surface faces approximately north to east. Erosion at the surface, facilitated by down-cutting from streams, moved the cliff in the direction of the dip thus exposing more tough Silurian dolomite and limestone. The cliff grew in height as it migrated.

Like most of Canada, the story of the Niagara Escarpment is primarily a story about the constructive and destructive powers of ice.

Glacial lobes[2] moved through southern Ontario several times; the most recent or Wisconsinan stage was effective at redistributing the handiwork of its predecessors. Deep sea sediment cores indicate that as many as twenty glacial episodes have affected North America over the last two to three million years. Although we know very little about the earliest glacial advances, we do know that the current landscape of southern Ontario is still primarily a product of the Wisconsinan glaciers. Like a giant Etch-a-Sketch, the Wisconsinan glaciers picked up everything in their paths, and shook them all around. Considering the thickness of the ice over the Escarpment, the landscape would have provided little resistance to the advancing sheets. The ice created a new baseline upon which other physical and ecological processes could act.

Two types of landscapes emerged from beneath the mountains of ice; one formed by deposition, the other by erosion. The land was either a sink or a source for the large volumes of glacial debris moved through the region. Evidence of glacial scouring can still be observed on the bedrock. Glacial meltwater streams cut through the Escarpment, while others cascaded over the cliffs to form incised valleys downstream. Some cliffs were separated from the main Escarpment and formed circular outliers (those sections of the Escarpment that are separated from the main cliff face) that are still evident at places like Cape Croker, Rattlesnake Point and Mono Cliffs. Some exposed bedrock was buried by unconsolidated glacial deposits or till. Till is carried by the glaciers and laid down when they stall or melt in situ. While the exposed dolomite of the Niagara Escarpment resisted the erosive powers of the glaciers, in some regions, such as Dufferin County, the exposed bedrock was buried by till and exposed cliff faces are virtually absent.

The Niagara Escarpment emerged as a bedrock feature from beneath the Wisconsinan Ice Sheet after the first ice-free areas were exposed close to 13,000 years ago. Within a thousand years, the ice sheet lay just north of Manitoulin Island. The meltwater was channelled east and water levels in the Great Lakes basin were relatively low. Most of the northern Escarpment, however, remained under the waters of glacial Lake Algonquin. The depressed land had yet to

A large plain separates the cliffs of Mount Nemo (shown here) from Rattlesnake Point, near Milton, Ontario.

recover from the weight of thousands of years of overlying ice. In some areas, the meltwater removed (in some cases catastrophically) overlying glacial drift and exposed the rock below. Eventually the land rebounded as water levels dropped and subsequently exposed areas of the Niagara Escarpment that were previously underwater. Variable rates of inflow from the north, coupled with variations in the direction and speed at which water could be drained into the St. Lawrence River, led to wild fluctuations in Great Lakes water levels over the next few thousand years. During these times, sections of the Escarpment were repeatedly exposed and inundated with water. The elevated middle portions of the Escarpment were least affected, but on the Bruce Peninsula the last flooding event occurred only 7,000 years ago. Lake levels continued to fluctuate (and continue to fluctuate today), but by 3,500 years ago, the peninsula looked very similar to the landform that we see today.

The Escarpment itself has been doing battle with a broad suite of physical forces over the last 15,000 years. Initially, glacial erosion removed overlying bedrock exposing grey and blue-grey dolomitic limestones and dolostones. Most of the original steepening of the exposed bedrock resulted from direct contact with glacial ice. Large influxes of cold glacial meltwater into the Great Lakes Basin prevented the climate from warming too rapidly. The discovery of periglacial features such as protalus ramparts indicate that permanent

snow packs persisted for hundreds of years along the base of the cliffs. These ramparts, or slopes, developed at the bottom of talus slopes and formed when rockfall hit the snow or ice. The debris rolled downslope and accumulated as a steep, rocky ridge. Meltwater channels also shaped cliff faces by cutting through them and creating a series of waterfalls, bedrock outliers and incised valleys. Drastic changes in postglacial lake levels completely inundated some faces, only to expose them again hundreds of years later. Wave-cut stacks or flowerpots, archways, sea caves and undercut cliffs were created where water interacted directly with the cliff face.

The effects of wave action have separated this stack or flowerpot from the Escarpment on Flowerpot Island.

It has been argued that the Niagara Escarpment talus may be a relict feature that developed shortly following deglaciation. Most undercut Escarpment cliffs were created by glacial ice, wave erosion at the cliff base or increased freeze-thaw activity brought on by severe climatic conditions at the end of the last glacial advance. Therefore, most of the talus formed 10,000 to 15,000 years ago. Undercutting has been minimal over the last few thousand years.

A limestone quarry used for the production of cut stone. Courtesy of the Esquesing Historical Society.

Frost does not penetrate more than four centimetres into the cliff face under present climatic conditions, which is unlikely to account for the large boulders that lie in the talus below many cliffs. One section of cliff face around Barrow Bay has previously been described as unstable because it has a high proportion of freshly fractured rock in the talus and there are several large, steep talus cones at the cliff base. However, the oldest living tree along the entire Niagara Escarpment is rooted under a huge overhang at this site! We are not implying that significant rock fall events do not occur along the Niagara Escarpment. We have seen the evidence for recent rock fall at several cliffs including Halfway Log Dump, Purple Valley and Rattlesnake Point, but as an entity, the Niagara Escarpment is not a naturally unstable feature of the landscape anymore.

The last one hundred years in the Escarpment's history, however, has brought about noticeable change. At first the European expansion into southern Ontario had little influence on the Escarpment, and it persisted on the landscape as it had for thousands of years. Even while the rest of the Ontario's natural landscape was being dismantled, the ancient cliff forest flourished. The construction boom that accompanied the migration of Canada's populace off farms and into urban centres, however, increased the demand for limestone as a natural resource. Limestone was cut for building stone and many of the oldest stone buildings in southern Ontario were

MILL & LIME KILN LIMEHOUSE ONT.

Lime was once in heavy demand for building construction and limestone was quarried at several locations along the Niagara. This mill and lime kiln operation was located near Limehouse. Courtesy of the Esquesing Historical Society.

built from Niagara Escarpment limestone – from turn-of-the century farmhouses to townhouses and homes in neighbouring cities such as Hamilton and Toronto.

Lime, a basic ingredient in mortar and plaster, was also heavily in demand. In the 1880s, every new stone or brick home contained large amounts of lime, which was produced by burning limestone at high temperatures. Quarries along the Niagara Escarpment extracted the rock that fuelled this boom. The cliff was broken into sections known as benches, using dynamite placed inside holes drilled into the rock. The benches were then broken into smaller pieces by men wielding sledge hammers. Two-wheeled horse-drawn carts hauled the limestone to open lime kilns fed by wood fuel twenty-four hours a day, seven days a week, to reach temperatures surpassing 1800°F. Thirty-six hours later, the "draw" of lime was loaded directly into "tips" or rail-cars. The lime was weighed, cooled and loaded into boxcars for transportation. By the mid-20th century, the popularity of quarried stone waned, lime production ceased altogether and crushed gravel took over as the dominant limestone product along the Niagara Escarpment.

Escarpment cliffs have also been destroyed for safety reasons. In 1959, the Niagara Parks Commission perceived overhangs as potential hazards, and had Ontario Hydro blast them in the Niagara Glen area of the Niagara Gorge. In the ensuing decades, the Commission blasted many other cliff faces in the gorge to ensure visitor safety. Other Escarpment cliffs have also been blasted to make way for ski resorts and highway construction.

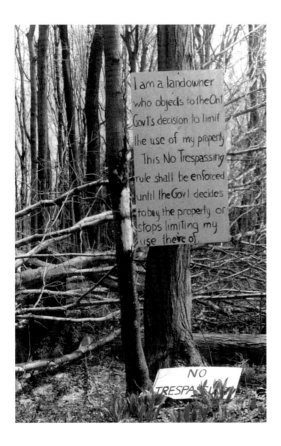

The Niagara Escarpment Plan has met with considerable opposition over the years especially by landowners who felt it infringed on their property rights. Courtesy of the Niagara Escarpment Commission.

While preserving the Niagara Escarpment is still an ongoing battle and corporate interests are still trying to stick their greedy fingers into the pie, popular public opinion has shifted to one of conservation and aesthetics. As the rest of southern Ontario's more accessible natural landscapes fell to the axe or plough, the importance of the Niagara Escarpment's natural corridors increased in the public eye. There was an outcry in the late sixties when a visible escarpment cliff face, near Milton and just north of the busy Highway 401, was dynamited and breached to facilitate access to a gravel pit. At the time, many people were unaware the Niagara Escarpment was not protected from development. The political climate was right for the implementation of a plan to ensure the protection of the Niagara Escarpment.

In 1973, the Niagara Escarpment Planning and Development Act was enacted by the Government of Ontario. The Act called for the establishment of the Niagara Escarpment Commission to design a plan that would impose developmental controls over escarpment lands. Any development within designated Niagara Escarpment zones would have to be judged on its compatibility with the goals and objectives of a Niagara Escarpment Plan: the principal goal being to maintain the Escarpment and the lands in its vicinity as a continuous natural environment. Input was encouraged through written comments and almost one hundred public meetings. While the majority of comments were favourable, there was a considerable amount of opposition to the plan. Most municipalities thought the plan area was too large, and eventually it was cut by seventy per cent of its former size. Many citizens saw the plan as a threat to their individual rights and freedoms. Written comments received included the following diatribe: "We do not want any part of the NEC, nor do we want strangers tramping over our land. The sooner the Commission is disbanded, the better off we will be."[3] Another individual, alarmingly, wrote, "I was sick with disgust, for you and the rest of the members

Cedars cling to the cliff edge on Old Baldy in the Beaver Valley, near Kimberly , Ontario.

A sailboat seeks santuary in the calm waters of Wingfield Basin at Cabot Head on the Bruce Peninsula.

of your board for the foul and ignorant proposals that you are trying to force on people....There is no reason why we who have purchased property, should be forced to give city people, who are too cheap to buy their own, access to ours....We will also shoulder arms if necessary to enforce our rights as owners of our lands!!"[4] Despite the opposition, the first Niagara Escarpment Plan was completed in 1985.

Ice, water and gravity have had a significant impact on the shape and form of the Niagara Escarpment over millions of years. We think of the series of cliffs that we recognize as the Niagara Escarpment as *The Escarpment,* but in actuality this chunk of rock has been squeezed, washed and crushed many times since it was first exposed at the surface of the earth. It has assumed many different forms in a number of locations. In the short term, the Niagara Escarpment isn't going anywhere and it persists today in a landscape otherwise devoid of exposed rock. The relentless pressures of human development, however, may be the most imposing and formidable force in the Escarpment's long history.

CHAPTER 2

EASTERN WHITE CEDAR

How little I know of that arbor vitae when I have heard only what science can tell me. It is but a word, it is not a tree of life. But there are twenty words for the tree and its different parts which the Indian gave, which are not in our botanies, which imply a more practical and vital science. He used it every day. He was well acquainted with its wood, its bark and its leaves.[1]
Henry David Thoreau

Until twenty years ago, eastern white cedar (also, or more properly known as arbor vitae) was regarded as a tree species inhabiting lowland areas such as swamps, stream banks and lakeshores as well as limestone pavements or rock outcrops. It was also considered by many to be a short-lived pioneer tree species of disturbed land. Age limits had previously been reported as 400 years. We now know that eastern white cedar growing on cliff faces can reach ages surpassing 1,500 years and that it is one of only a handful of species that exhibit such longevity under adverse conditions.

While uncommon in most trees, maximum ages approaching one thousand years are more common in the Cupressaceae, the taxonomic family that includes eastern white cedar, giant arbour-vitae or *Thuja occidentalis*. Most true cedars, cypresses and junipers are also members of the Cupressaceae. The only other member of the genus *Thuja* in North America is the western red cedar or *Thuja plicata*. In the temperate rain forests of the Pacific Northwest western red cedar can reach heights up to sixty metres and surpass five metres in diameter.

The scaly leaves of eastern white cedar are unique amongst trees in Ontario.

At high altitudes, however, it may be only a small tree or shrub. The maximum lifespan of western red cedar is thought to be over a thousand years.

Eastern white cedar on the other hand rarely attains sizes greater than a metre in diameter or more than twenty metres in height. It grows at altitudes between sea level and 1,300 metres, although it only grows at these higher elevations in upstate New York on sites where water flows directly over rock. It commonly grows with eastern hemlock, eastern white pine, yellow birch and silver or red maple or in pure stands on dry sites. In level-ground habitats, eastern white cedars have a distinctive conical shape. In open areas, living branches extend to the ground, but, in forests, the bottom branches are either absent or dead. Living branches tend to dip downwards and then grow skywards near the tip. The leaves are unusual – scale-like, flat, lance-shaped and yellowish-green in colour – and like humans they become more bronze as the growing season progresses.

Cedars grow almost exclusively on alkaline soils enriched with calcium. Lateral movement of water is also critical for eastern white cedar stands, and the water needs to be enriched with high concentrations of oxygen and essential nutrients. A good flow rate is found in many typical eastern white cedar habitats including lakeshores, wetlands, sand dunes, rocky outcrops or cliffs. They are often found growing on shallow soils because cedar is very tolerant of both short-term droughts and flooding. Like other trees it avoids significant drought injury by taking advantage of water when it is plentiful, but closing its stomata (small openings in the leaves through which gases pass) for extended periods of time in response to water stress.

The sex life of the white cedar is probably more interesting than you might think. Cedars are monoecious plants, which means they have both the male and female structures required for reproduction on the same plant. If they were human, they would all be hermaphrodites. Sexual reproduction may start in trees as young as five or six years, but often doesn't start until trees are much older. Peak seed production occurs after seventy-five years. The oldest known living cedars have full complements of seed cones and these seeds are as viable as seeds from the youngest trees.

Cedar cones mature in the fall during which time their seeds are dispersed by the wind.

The male is represented on the tree by pollen cones. These cones, approximately four millimetres in length, develop near the base of branchlets. The pollen is released in the spring, when it hopes to find its way to female or seed cones at branchlet tips. The pollen cones and seed cones are usually on different branches. Seeds develop over the summer and the cones ripen between August and September. In autumn, the cones dry, seeds are released and then scattered by the wind. A typical eastern white cedar can yield up to 260,000 seeds. That's a big family! The seeds tend to fall within fifty to sixty metres of the mother tree although seeds produced on cliff-face trees may be carried much further.

In a level-ground forest, the successful germination of cedar seedlings is dependent on the availability of logs and gaps in the forest canopy associated with them. They are also dependent on temperatures above 18°C to germinate. Thankfully, for the sake of earth's other species, only a small percentage of seeds actually germinate!

This moss-covered rock, which rises above the leaf litter on the forest floor, provides a suitable substrate for the germination of cedar seeds.

This mature cedar was once just a seedling on a stump.

Mortality is high amongst cedar seedlings as they typically germinate on substrates such as logs and moss that are prone to drying out as the growing season progresses. Even fewer will survive more than a couple years. On the cliff face, where competition from other plants is minimal, successful germination is dependent on the seed finding a suitable crack or crevice.

Surprisingly, this is only one way that eastern white cedars can propagate themselves. Eastern white cedar (and a few related species in North America) can simply skip sexual reproduction altogether. How do they do that? They simply produce clones of themselves. This is known as layering. Stems or branches of eastern white cedar are capable of producing roots when moisture conditions are favourable and the tree is in contact with the ground. Sometimes the side branches of a tree that is blown over grows upward. The increased weight causes the original stem to descend to the soil surface. Once contact is made, a new set of roots may develop and the tree can function as if nothing had happened. Except that the cedar looks more like a pretzel now than a tree. This trick also allows cedars thrown by the wind or tipped over by an unstable substrate to establish new sets of roots.

Asexual reproduction through layering is a handy mechanism that allows cedars to persist in swamps where their shallow roots make them vulnerable to falling or tipping over. This process is especially prevalent along cliff edges where shallow soils make the trees vulnerable to wind damage. It also allows cedars to adjust to environmental change and reproduce even after conditions are no longer ideal for sexual reproduction. If there is a habitat shift (perhaps precipitated by industrious beavers!) from swamp to bog (an atypical environment for cedars), then cedar stands may persevere even after the new habitat is invaded by another tree species such as black spruce. Layering also enables cedars to reproduce under dense shade where seedlings wouldn't survive. It provides them with reproductive flexibility. Layering allows shade-tolerance in a normally shade-intolerant species. On the cliff face, layering is less common because trees become established on small ledges, and in cracks and crevices. An unstable tree is apt to hang upside-down or fall completely into the talus rather than find a suitable neighbouring site on which to produce a new set of roots.

Cedars are at home in swamps, along lake margins, such as here at Crawford Lake north of Burlington, and on cliffs but only on cliffs do they reach ages surpassing 500 years.

Compared with many of its companion species in central North America, eastern white cedar has relatively few enemies. Cedar is affected by few serious diseases and they are relatively free of insect damage. The main pests are ants and Arborvitae leaf miners. Ants such as *Formica exsectoides* may kill small cedars, while carpenter ants work within the heartwood of living cedars causing instability in the tree. Arborvitae leaf miners (*Argyresthia thuiella* being the most common species in Ontario) are small caterpillars that feed within the leaves causing the tips of the branches to turn brown. They start on the outside of the tree, eventually working their way towards the trunk. Cedars can survive losing up to 80% of their leaves to leaf miners. The Cedar-tree Borer (*Semanotus ligneus*) and the Northern Cedar Bark Beetle (*Phloeosinus canadensis*) will tunnel into wood, but they feed primarily on dying cedar trees and are not considered a serious threat to healthy trees. The Japanese Cedar Longhorned Beetle is a pest that was accidentally introduced into North America in 1997 and has been found on eastern white cedar. Adults colonize weak cedars and the larvae bore into wood, but apparently cause only minimal damage.

Other insects sometimes found on white cedar include the aphid (*Cinara cupressi*), the bagworm (*Thyridopteryx ephemeraeformis*), sawflies (*Monoctenus* sp.) and several species of loopers, but epidemics are unknown and they are not thought to cause serious injury to the trees. Rare diseases such as leaf blight (*Fabrella thujina*) and juniper blight (*Phomopsis juniperovora*) can cause premature leaf browning and

This 600-year-old cedar is still alive despite the erosion of the rock surface upon which it was growing.

shedding. Phytophtora root rot can also cause roots to decay in moist environments while various butt-rot fungi can infect the cedars. None of these pests or diseases are widespread enough to pose a significant threat to white cedar populations.

Eastern white cedar is a favourite browse food for some mammal species, especially in winter. Deer favour cedars by a wide margin over other commonly available wintertime browse species. When given the option of browsing cedar over twenty other browse species, deer made cedar 90% of their diet. Deer can account for significant mortality of the youngest trees because eastern white cedar is such a slow-growing species. Deer also frequent white cedar stands because they impose important winter thermal cover. Porcupines also feed on cedar foliage in the winter particularly in the tree crowns. In some cases, this can kill the main axis of the tree. Rodents can account for significant losses of seedlings, while the red squirrel harvests branchlets with cones from mature trees in autumn. Snowshoe hares are also heavy browsers and the northern pileated woodpecker bores large holes in mature cedars in their quest for carpenter ants. Humans pose an indirect hazard to white cedars because of roadway construction. White cedar is negatively affected by road salt.

While some northern tree species are relatively resistant to fire (some are dependent on fire for reproduction!), eastern white cedar is not. A ground fire easily damages their shallow root systems and the shaggy oil-rich bark is flammable. Excessive heat alone is fatal to these trees and large cedars may survive only if ground cover is relatively sparse. The oldest cedar trees persist where fire is excluded. Eastern white cedar is one of the first species to colonize sites razed by fire and many cedar forests became established after major fires. An intense fire that destroys the surface organic horizon, however, may delay colonization for some time.

The Migration Northwards

Although popular as an ornamental tree, eastern white cedar occurs naturally throughout central and eastern Canada and throughout the northern United States. It occurs as far west as Manitoba, including

isolated populations along the shores of Cedar Lake (not surprisingly!) and the northern shores of Lake Winnipeg and Lake
Winnepegosis. Its distribution is continuous between Winnipeg and
southern Nova Scotia, as far north as James Bay and as far south as
Chicago, Illinois; Flint, Michigan; the Hudson River Valley in New
York and southern Maine. Below this range, eastern white cedar persists as far south as Virginia and Tennessee in small isolated populations. It has not always been this way.

Some remarkable details on the recent history of this species have
been uncovered by Dr. Gary Walker of Appalachian State University,
who has studied cedar populations in North Carolina and Tennessee.
Walker found high levels of genetic diversity in populations of white
cedar on the Eastern Highland Rim of Tennessee but low genetic
diversity at other sites with a history of disturbance. This led him to
conclude that the Highland Rim populations were relict stands from
a once-continuous distribution at the height of the last glacial maximum
20,000 years ago. When the continent warmed some 14,000 years ago,
the glaciers receded, and the eastern white cedars migrated northwards
along river valleys and back into present-day Canada. These pioneers
became the forefathers of populations now prevalent throughout the
Great Lakes region. By 12,500 years ago white cedar had moved northwards into southwestern Ontario and cedar occupied the shores of the
Champlain Sea – a postglacial body of water that covered much of northeastern North America 12,000 to 10,000 years ago. A leafy twig collected
from sediments on Manitoulin Island reveals that cedar had migrated
there by at least 10,000 years ago. The southern populations fragmented
about 12,000 years ago and became isolated stands by 8,000 years ago.

Today, white cedar is abundant within its range where it is perhaps
the most recognizable and easily identifiable tree species. Ironically,
cedar in Tennessee is now at the extreme southern extension of its
range where it only occupies steep north-facing limestone slopes or
cliffs. These cliffs provided white cedar with a refuge at the height of
the last glaciation and possibly saved the species from extinction.
Here, isolated glacial relict plant communities on cliffs are tangible
reminders of the widespread havoc that ice sheets wreaked on the
distribution of the continent's flora, including eastern white cedar.

CHAPTER 3

THE GREAT MEDICINE TREE

I wish I could go with you. If I could drink cedar-tea
I should soon be rid of my rheumatism.[1]
Cyrus G. Pringle, 1911

From its early beginnings colonizing the postglacial landscape of east-central North America, white cedar was part of the cultural traditions of the region's First Nations' peoples. It is an integral part of the teachings of the Medicine Wheel – a symbol that teaches a holistic view of the world from a Native perspective. These teachings include concepts dealing with the four seasons, the four directions, the four colours (yellow, red, black and white, which represent the four colours of humankind) and the four medicines (tobacco, sage, sweetgrass and cedar). As one of the four medicines, white cedar played a central role in the cosmological world of pre-contact Ojibwa and Potawatomi who referred to themselves as the Anishnaabeg or "true people." The Anishnaabeg were simply the descendents of the first peoples created in their own mythology.

The Anishnaabeg perceived the world as flat with various realms of the cosmos stacked upon each other above and below the flat earth. This physical world was occupied by plants, animals and a menagerie of supernatural creatures. These included the windigo

The four colours and medicines of importance to southern Ontario's First Nations People (from a display at a reconstructed 15th Century Iroquoian village at Crawford Lake Conservation Area).

(a cannibal giant), the bagudzinishinabe (little wild people) and the maymayggayshi (mischievous water elves). From four to sixteen other realms filled their cosmos including the visible atmosphere occupied by the birds and the animiki (or thunderbirds) who caused thunder by flapping their wings and hurling lightning from their talons. The moon, the sun and the stars occupied the upper sky or sky vault that was home to many different spirits. These included those spirits associated with the cardinal directions, winds and the cycle of the seasons. The sky vault was also the land beyond death where the dead lived in villages free from deprivation.

Below the flat earth there was a dark and dangerous underworld inhabited by deadly creatures such as the michipishiew (underwater panther) and the mishikinebik (serpents with horns). Occasionally these creatures rose to the surface through caves, crevices and whirlpools to wreak havoc. The michipishiew was particularly unfriendly and caused violent storms on the lakes by thrashing its huge tail.

Contact between the different realms was not only dangerous but mystical as well. Dreams, death and shamanistic spirit voyaging were all thought to involve exchanges of mind, body or spirit from one realm to another. Snakes, toads, frogs, otters and turtles were travellers between the earth or water and the underworld and were beheld with magical significance.

The only commonality amongst the various layers of the Anishnaabeg cosmos was the great medicine tree. It was rooted in the underworld and like a great spike burst upwards through the many layers of the cosmic cake and into the sky vault, thus allowing light to reach the earth. Light is symbolic of wisdom and knowledge and both light and the great medicine tree were known by the same Ojibwa word – *gijik* – the eastern white cedar.

TEAS, PASTES AND POULTICES

Iroquois in Quebec were the first to show Europeans the eastern white cedar. Although the exact tree species used is still debated, eastern white cedar is cited as having saved the lives of French explorer Jacques Cartier and his crew when their ship was icebound in Quebec in the winter of 1535–36. Cartier had already lost 25 crewmen to scurvy when a group of local Indians showed them how to prepare a tea by boiling the bark and leaves of a tree known locally as "annedda." Cartier referred to it as the tree of life or Arbre de vie (arbor vitae) since the Vitamin C in the tea saved his crew from imminent death.

Thuja occidentalis is still referred to as arbor vitae although eastern white cedar is most popular name used in Canada, while northern white cedar is popular in the United States. The genus name "Thuja" comes from the Greek words *thoun* or *thuia*, which refers to an aromatic African tree commonly burnt in religious ceremonies. *Thuia* also became the word meaning "to sacrifice" and "to bear scent." The word *occidentalis* means western and refers to the tree as a New World species. Other common names for this species include: eastern arbor vitae, northern arbor vitae, swamp cedar, eastern thuja, balai, American arbor vitae, American cedar, Michigan white cedar, New Brunswick cedar, Atlantic red cedar, yellow cedar, false white cedar, livstrad, tuya and hackmatack!

The reputation of the cedar as the great medicine tree was well founded as its bark and leaves were used to cure dozens of ailments. Native North Americans utilized virtually every part of the white cedar as ingredients in medicine. The most commonly prepared remedies were teas brewed from the bark and leaves. In 1557, André Thévet reported that Natives in the Gulf of St. Lawrence "take the leaves of a tree which is very like the cedars….and take the juice which they drink. And it is not to be doubted that in twenty four hours, they are not as sick, even if it is inveterate within the body, that this drink cures them…"[2] The Ojibwa drank teas made from white cedar leaf tips to treat ailments including coughs, colds and headaches. The Chippewa mixed the leaves with hop-hornbeam to produce a type of cough syrup. In his book, *Secrets of the Native American Herbal Remedies*, Anthony J. Cichoke listed the following white cedar tea recipe as a cough and cold remedy:

> 2 cups white cedar leaf tips
> 30 drops echinacea tincture
> 20 drops wild indigo root tincture

> Combine the above ingredients and take half a cup at
> a time, hot, up to three times a day.[3]

Cedar tea was also thought to purify the blood and ironically, it was reported as a cure for both dysentery and constipation! The River Desert Algonquin of western Quebec used a tea made from the cones to treat colic in babies, while Menominee Indians in Wisconsin treated suppressed menstruation with a tea prepared from the tree's dried inner bark. Mohawk women were also known to drink a tea made from cedar leaves for forty days following childbirth. It increased perspiration that in turn was thought to increase the secretion of milk. The River Desert Algonquin also used the leaves in a steam bath for women recovering from childbirth and to treat colds and fevers. The tea has also been used traditionally to treat gout, scurvy and rheumatic symptoms.

Other reported uses of *Thuja* include the treatment of "bloody flux." Native populations of northern Quebec filled a bladder enema with a cedar juice concoction prepared by boiling the extremities of cedar branches. Post-contact Chippewa in Michigan believed that burning white cedar twigs disinfected their homes of contagious diseases such as smallpox introduced by Europeans. Further west, the Chippewa burned cedar to alleviate back pain. The Menominee used herbal steams made from cedar for skin ailments and to revive the unconscious. The Potawatomi burned the leaves for similar effect. Cedar gum was also used by the Maliseet to fill tooth cavities. This reduced the pain but unfortunately killed the tooth.

Eastern white cedar pastes and poultices were prepared to treat maladies externally. A salve boiled from a mixture of crushed white cedar leaves and grease provided temporary relief from rheumatic pains. A similar mixture was applied to hands and feet to reduce swelling. A poultice made from a mixture of polypody fern, cedar cones and warm milk reportedly relieved body pains in the area in which it was applied. The poultice was thought to burn like fire and a cloth was required between the body and the mixture to prevent the afflicted from being scorched or burnt on the skin! The Menominee Indians eased swelling by applying a poultice prepared from dried, powdered cedar leaves mixed with a powdered fungus. Some Algonquin Indians rubbed powdered white cedar directly onto skin affected by rashes and skin irritations. Cichoke reported that the following wash could treat the fungal skin infection that causes athlete's foot:

> 4 teaspoons big sagebrush root
> 4 teaspoons white cedar leaf tips
> 2 cups water
> Combine the herbs in a nonmetallic container and
> cover with the water. Soak for 8 hours; strain. Apply
> the liquid topically several times a day.[4]

An unusual use of cedar involved the application of cedar (and hazel) charcoal to treat headaches, rheumatism and body pain. The Chippewa took a small quantity of the charcoal and mixed it with equal proportions of dried bear gall bladder or bear fat and water. The mixture was then placed on the affected part and worked into the skin using needles. A diagnostic feature that this remedy had been applied was the presence of dark spots on the temples of affected persons. Cedar charcoal was even used to whiten teeth and treat bad breath!

Eastern white cedar is still used as a natural remedy for a number of ailments. A list of ailments reportedly eased by treatment with eastern white cedar (in one form or another) encompasses all manner of the human condition. These include: prostate problems, bedwetting, haemorrhoids, typhus, toothaches, depression, amnesia, fainting, venereal warts, inflammation of the ear, scleritis (inflammation of the white of the eye), iritis (inflammation of the iris), nasal polyps, catarrh (inflammation of the air passages of the head and throat), skin tumours, haemorrhaging, plantar warts, burns, worms, muscle pain, rhinitis (inflammation of the mucous membrane of the nose), itching, urinary diseases, tissue degeneration, shortness of breath, pharyngitis (inflammation at the back of the mouth), angina and blepharitis (inflammation of the eyelids)!

Today, *Thuja occidentalis* is sold by most commercial homeopathic retailers. Extractions of cedar are sold as pellets, salves and as tinctures. One retailer claims that *Thuja occidentalis* can be used to treat the following: amenorrhea, arthritis, burns, catarrh, the common cold, condyloma, coughs, depurative, excrescence, fevers, gout, headaches, orthopedic ailments, pain rheumatism, scurvy, skin ailments, skin fungal infections, swelling, toothaches, warts and women's ailments. It is claimed to be any and all of the following: an adjuvant, alterative, analgesic, antirheumatic, antiseptic, astringent, bactericide, blood cleanser, counterirritant, diaphoretic, disinfectant, diuretic, emmenagogue, expectorant, fenrifuge, irritant, panacea, stimulant and sudorific! Eastern white cedar is also one of four ingredients in the popular herbal medication Esberitox. Esberitox also includes extractions of *Echinacea purpurea* (purple coneflower), *Echinacea pallida* (pale coneflower) and *Baptisia tinctoria* (wild indigo) and is championed as being a booster of the immune system. Although some clinical studies have been performed, the results are inconclusive on the benefits of Esberitox and other isolates of *Thuja occidentalis* in fighting breast cancer, leukemia and immune deficiency syndromes.

Jeff Matheson stands above a massive 630-year-old cedar growing out a cave on the northern tip of the Bruce Peninsula.

Whether *Thuja occidentalis* can be used as an effective treatment for certain conditions, however, is still unknown. In high dosages, the oil extracted from cedar leaves can cause convulsions and has led to fatalities. Its role as an abortifacient (agent causing abortion) is also well-known. Charles F. Millspaugh in his 1892 book, *American Medicinal Plants,* wrote that the "main action of Thuja is on the genitourinary organs, copious and frequent urination…the sexual appetite is suppressed."[5] Indeed, the seemingly contradictory role of *Thuja* extractives was plainly stated by Bocclerus (in Millspaugh's book) who said that, "while the excessive chilliness, heat, and profuse sweat, point to a remedy often in intermittent fevers…the peculiar action of this drug is one difficult of explanation."[6] In 1876, Dr. Richard Hughes summarized these effects by stating that *Thuja* caused, "copious and frequent urination; burning in several parts of the mucous tract; pains of various kinds in the penis; inflammation of the prepuce and glans; ulcers, tubercles, and other excrescences on the sexual organs, with itching and profuse sweating; and, in the female, leucorrhoea. The sexual appetite was depressed, and the cata-menia retarded. Burning, itching, swelling, and mucous discharge occurred at the anus; and on the skin generally, but especially in the ano-genital region, tubercles and warts were developed. In the neigh-bouring mucous membranes similar phenomena appeared, but nat-urally of moister character."[7] When Henry Thoreau heard that "lumberers" prepared arbor-vitae teas to keep them strong and healthy, he wrote that he had "no wish to repeat the experiment. It had too medicinal a taste for my palate"![8] Considering Hughes' com-ments, Thoreau may have not known how lucky he really was!!

Clearly the reported health benefits of *Thuja occidentalis* are con-tradictory. Thujone, the main constituent of the volatile oil in *Thuja* is certainly toxic in high concentrations. It was thujone that was the principal component of absinthe, a popular drink in the late 19th cen-tury, particularly in France. Unfortunately, the symptoms of absinthe overindulgence far surpassed the slurred speech, red cheeks and lack of judgment normally associated with the excess consumption of alcohol. Absinthe victims experienced terrifying hallucinations and appeared to be in a daze after prolonged sessions with the green drink. Chronic drinkers such as Vincent van Gogh were said to have "absinthism." Van Gogh was addicted to absinthe and this addiction aggravated his psychoses. His suicide may have been triggered by fits of hallucinations brought on by his absinthism. Van Gogh's doctor planted a *Thuja* on his grave even though *Thuja occidentalis* was not the principal source of thujone for absinthe in France [that being worm-wood (*Artemisia absinthium*) and Roman wormwood (*Artemisia pontica*)].

Eastern white cedar wood is also known to be toxic to sawmill workers who are exposed to it on a regular basis. Occupational asthma is found amongst workers in mills who are affected by cedar wood dust in the air. The agent responsible for this toxicity is plicatic acid, although the mechanisms by which this toxic effect is accomplished are unknown. Exposure to plicatic acid can cause or exacerbate medical conditions such as asthma, rhinitis or conjunctivitis (inflammation of the mucous membranes of the eyelids). It leads to the sensitization of the immune system to foreign substances.

It is likely that the relative toxicity or beneficial qualities of cedar are a function of the concentration of the dose. It is unlikely that the aboriginal peoples of the Great Lakes region continued to use cedar as a remedy without repeated improvements to some aspects of the human condition.

Purification

The practical application of eastern white cedar as a living pharmacy meant that the tree has special importance to the Native populations of central North America. Cedar is revered as a sacred gift from the spirits of nature. Potawatomi oral tradition relates the story of how cedar was brought to their people. It involves the story of six men who yearned to visit the Sun. They called the tribe together, informed them of their plan and warned them that they might not return for a very long time, if at all. They headed east and eventually found the spot where the Sun rose. In the morning, they caught hold of the Sun. Each man asked it for something that they could use to make their people happy. One man requested everlasting life because he wanted to help his people for as long as the earth would last. The Sun told him on his journey back that he would suddenly turn into something that never dies. His name would be Cedar Tree and he would remain forever with all the nations and peoples of the earth. "You will be the first one that they use in their feasts and all people will think of you as holy," said the Sun.

His brother did not want to leave his side and therefore made the same request. The Sun obliged and told him that he too would be everlasting and change at the same time as his brother. When the Sun reached the west, the men hopped off and thanked it for its blessings. On their way back the first brother suddenly announced, "Here is where I am to stay!" When the others looked back they saw a cedar tree. "Take my leaves and use them for incense at your ceremonies," it said, "and call the cedar tree your nephew when you speak of it." The second brother stopped and turned into a great boulder. "Heat this stone when you are sick and use me in your sweat lodges when you purify yourselves with the cedar," it said. It also urged the others to visit them to pray and make offerings of tobacco.[9] Even today, cedar is burned to relieve grief during Native funeral rites because of its reputation as the tree of immortality.

Eastern white cedar has thus been incorporated into many Native North American ceremonies and rituals. The Ojibwa and the Potawatomi burn cedar wood during smudging ceremonies. Participants purify themselves by wafting smoke over their person. Sacred objects are purified in a similar manner. Purification ceremonies are especially important during medicine lodge ceremonies. The Dahcotah burn the leaves of white cedar to destroy the supernatural powers of people who dislike them. White cedar is regarded as wahkun or as a spiritual plant that protects against evil and wards off the danger from lightning. Lightning is controlled by the Thunderbirds; who take the form of hawks or eagles and were some of the first spirits created on earth. In the presence of humans, however, they appear as bald men with war clubs and wreaths of white cedar. Inhaling the smoke of burning cedar chips is also thought to provide protection from bad dreams and to induce and strengthen psychic powers.

Outside of purification and smudging ceremonies, white cedar is thought to possess other mystical properties. A three-pronged cedar stick stuck prongs up into the ground is supposed to protect a home from evil, and cedar chips in your wallet are supposed to attract money. White cedar has even become an integral part of ceremonies amongst some immigrant populations as white cedar switches are an important part of sauna rituals for Finnish Americans. Eastern white cedar is also an ingredient in some witchcraft recipes – added whenever the recipe calls for Kronos' blood!

LEGEND OF GLOOSKAP

Considering the spiritual and medicinal importance of white cedar to the First Nations peoples, did they attribute any particular significance to the slow-growing cedars protruding from cliff faces or rock outcrops? Were they aware of the connection between the unusual morphology of white cedar growing in these rocky habitats and extreme age? Could they have known that a small twisted cedar on a cliff face could be much older than a large cedar growing in the forest above? We discovered a Mi'Knaw story about Glooskap, their spiritual master, that seems to indicate that this was the case. This story was published by Charles T. Leland in 1884 and based on notes taken by Baptist missionary Reverend Silas T. Rand who worked among the Mi'Knaw First Nation in Nova Scotia.[10]

Glooskap turning a man into a cedar tree. A woodcut from Charles Leland's 1884 book The Algonquin Legends of New England.

It was thought amongst the Mi' Kmaq that Glooskap could win the desires of the hearts of men. In Rand's version of the story, three brothers ventured out from their village to find Glooskap who lived on the island of Aja-lig-un-mechk. Eventually the brothers came to the island where they found an unusual man named Cuhkw (meaning earthquake). Cuhkw could travel underground and made all things quake in his presence. When they arrived, one brother told Glooskap that he wished to forever behold the beauty of the land. The second brother yearned to be taller than all others. The third wished he could forever be in good health and live to a very old age. When Glooskap heard the brothers' wishes, he instructed Cuhkw to plant all three with their feet in the ground. They instantly became cedar trees. With his roots in the ground, the first brother got his wish while Glooskap made the second brother grow exceedingly tall. Glooskap transformed the third brother "into an old gnarled and twisted cedar, with limbs growing out rough and ugly all the way from the bottom. "There," he said to the cedar tree, "I cannot say how

A twisted cedar stands guard over a dead relative on the cliff at Old Baldy in the Beaver Valley.

long you will live; only the Great Spirit above can tell that; but you will not be disturbed for a good while, as no one can have any object in cutting you down. You are yourself unfit for any earthly purpose, and the land around you is useless for cultivation. I think you will stand there for a long while."

CHAPTER 4

CANOES, POSTS AND PILES

The Canadians have a common saying, that "the white cedar will last for ever,
and will then serve for window-sashes!"[1]
Edward Allen Talbot, 1824

hile "forever" may be stretching the truth, eastern white cedar wood has developed a deserved reputation for its durability and resistance to decay. A number of studies led by E.A. Behr in the sixties and seventies found that while decay resistance varied within *Thuja*, on average it was more decay and termite resistant than wood from most other tree species and on par with western red cedar. Decay resistance is greatest in the heartwood (innermost non-conducting wood) of the tree just inside its boundary with the sapwood (living conducting wood found between the heartwood and the bark). We have observed this same phenomenon in dead cedars along the Niagara Escarpment. If rot is observed in the tree, it is often confined to the pith (or centre of the tree) and its outermost wood layers.

The principal enemies of decay in cedar are fungi with glamorous names like stringy-butt rot and brown-butt rot. We should be thankful that these aren't common maladies of the human condition! Decay is accelerated by contact with water and/or soil. Water

This submerged stump (still rooted in the rock) is all that remains of a cedar tree that grew in this spot thousands of years ago when water levels in Georgian Bay were much lower than they are today.
Photo by Bill Knudsen.

leaches out the compounds responsible for decay resistance allowing the decay fungi to move in and rot the wood. If the wood is kept dry and out of contact with soil, or away from the fungi that lead to decay, the wood can endure for thousands of years. We found intact 3,550 year-old (radiocarbon-dated) eastern white cedar wood in the rocky talus at the base of one cliff. Submerged cedar wood over 8,500 years in age has been found at a depth of ten metres in the waters of Georgian Bay. Both wood samples showed little evidence of structural change despite thousands of years of exposure to the elements.

Thuja wood is also extremely light-weight with an average density of 335 kg per cubic metre of wood. It is also very easy to split. Unfortunately, while both durable and light, eastern white cedar grows much slower than most other species and the trees are small in stature. The lumber is often very knotty. This is probably the reason why eastern white cedar is not one of the principal commercial lumber species in eastern North America today.

The aboriginal peoples of this continent, however, took full advantage of the unique properties of cedar and used it in all manners of construction. The most enduring image of the First Nations peoples is the cedarstrip canoe. Henry Hind described the construction of a cedarstrip canoe in his 1869 essays on the Dominion of Canada, "The framework consists of numerous single ribs or laths, bent like an ox-bow, and terminating in the gunwales; all which, with the bow and stern-post, are made of white cedar (*Thuya occidentalis*) the lightest and most durable wood our forest affords. The few bars which maintain the opposite gunwales in situ are of maple, elm, or ash – cedar not being strong enough – but they are attached, through holes bored in their ends, by a seizing of young roots, (instead of

The cedarstrip canoe was an essential form of transportation for eastern Canada's First Nations.

being framed in) so that they can be readily replaced."[2] Spruce roots were boiled and used to attach the white birch sheathing while a pitch made from resin and tallow was used to seal the seams and make it watertight. Sometimes white cedar bark was used for the sheathing if white birch was unavailable.

The cedarstrip canoe was the ideal vehicle for navigating the Canadian wilderness. Before rail lines and roads carved up the landscape, rivers provided the only viable transportation corridor between destinations. The canoes were lighter than any other vehicle of equal strength thus facilitating travel on dry land. Only half the crew was required to carry it, thus freeing hands for cargo. The elastic nature of the wood withstood moderate collisions or contact with rocks hidden from view and, if not, the repair shop was never more than half the width of the river or lake away! Better yet, the canoes also served as shelter at night. Hind writes, "every attempt to improve upon it, by substitution of tin or otherwise, has failed."[3]

Cedar stems and cedar bark were also popular construction materials because of their durability. They were used in the construction of palisades and permanent structures like longhouses. Sieur de Cadillac described the construction of dwellings by the Ottawa and the Huron at Mackinac and writes that they, "entwine with these large poles, crosspieces as thick as one's arm, and cover them from

Iroquoian longhouses were constructed almost entirely from white cedar. Even cedar bark was used to tie cedar posts together.

White cedar (background) is so durable that it was the principal wood used for posts, rails and fences (foreground). Cedar rail fences still dot the landscape of southern Ontario. Note the forest of cedars in the background.

top to bottom with the bark of fir trees or cedars, which they fasten to the poles and the cross branches."[4] Cedar bark was the most popular choice for covering all manner of dwellings although it was flammable, leaving entire collections of villagers vulnerable to fire. The stringy bark was also used to weave bags and make baskets and was stuffed into pillows and upholstery. It was rolled up to serve as torches and rubbed to a powder, ignited and used to start fires.

In winter, the Huron First Nation used cedar to construct a type of sledge known as an *arocha*. The *arocha* was constructed of long boards of cedar wood upon which the load was placed. It was then attached to their feet and pulled over the snow. The young branches were also used as brooms, and the twigs and leaves were used as green dyes for clothing and objects. Cedar boughs were also thought to ward off insects and the Huron slept on cedar boughs that were thought to repel snakes. The light cedar wood was favoured especially for armour and helmets, and cedar was often the wood of choice for arrow and spear shafts. The Huron made huge shields out of cedar that covered most of their bodies.

Like the First Nations peoples before them, the first settlers to the Great Lakes Lowlands took advantage of the robust and resilient white cedar wood – split-rail fences being the most obvious manifestation in southern Ontario. An 1863 lease signed between George Peavoy

This 1947 photograph shows a load of cedar destined to become fence posts. Courtesy of the Archives of Ontario: Department of Lands and Forests photographs of fire-fighting activities and fish hatcheries, RG1-610.

and Charles Connolly for the use of land in the Township of Erin in Wellington County, stipulated that ten acres of land be cleared each year for five years "and to fence with a lawful fence each ten acres into fields with cedar rails...and the cedar not required for rails to be piled unto piles."[5] In some areas cedar rail fences are still a prominent part of the rural landscape. Some fences have endured nearly 150 years of exposure to the elements but still serve as effective barriers for livestock. Unfortunately, not everyone was appreciative of their usefulness. Naturalist Philip Henry Gosse wrote in 1840 that "the white cedar... from the facility with which it is split, but chiefly from its great durability, almost incorruptibility...is in great request for the rails that compose those unsightly zigzag fences, so offensive to the eye of one accustomed to the verdant and blooming hedgerows of England."![6]

Gosse's disgust, however, did not limit eastern white cedar's popularity as the wood of choice for fence posts, pickets and rails. It was also popular for telegraph poles, shingles, siding, beams, docks, piers, railway ties and lime kilns. An intact tramway of cedar rails laid nearly fifty years prior at a now abandoned mill on the Bruce Peninsula was proclaimed by W. Sherwood Fox to be a "tribute to the workmen who laid them and to the lasting qualities of our native white cedar."[7] Fishermen discovered that the wood was great for building their boats and settlers used it for a wide variety of household

The varied appearance of four different cultivars of eastern white cedar.

items including pails, tubs, churns, sugar-making spiles and brooms because the wood became smoother and whiter with increased use.

Barns were also shingled with cedar. Cedar shingles was preferred habitat for several moss species. This layer of moss kept the barn dry because it absorbed moisture when it rained and expanded to seal cracks and holes. On dry days, farmers could look up to their roofs and see light through the cracks even though the barn interior was kept completely dry in wet weather. In 18th century United States, cedar was cut from swamps in New Jersey to meet the demand for cedar shingles. When the supply was exhausted, long-dead cedar trunks floated to the surface and they were in turn "mined" for shingles. The wood was dried and found to be equally effective. A layer of cedars nearly twelve feet deep was found in some of these swamps. This buried wood was used to construct the roof of Independence Hall in Philadelphia.

Eastern white cedar wood is still useful today for products that come in contact with water and soil, items such as: poles, posts, fencing, shingles, boats, particle board, boxes, crates and water tanks. It is the first choice for fence posts by most farmers, but the introduction of pressure-treated wood and chemical wood preservatives such as creosote, has limited the current usefulness of *Thuja* for railway ties, docks and piers. It is popular for log cabins because it is an efficient insulator, has a low shrinkage factor, and a low moisture content. The Forestry Division of the U.S. Department of Agriculture ranks it as one of the three best woods to use for exterior construction. The wood is used for fishnet floats and imitation minnows because of its lightness. One company claims their eastern white cedar cat scratching posts are ideal because "white cedar has the claw-pleasing roughness cats crave....so soft they can easily dig their claws in for maximum scratching exercise and satisfaction." No doubt! Extracts from *Thuja occidentalis* are also used in cleansers, disinfectants, hair products, insecticides, insect repellents, deodourizers, perfumes and soaps.

Thuja occidentalis (including its many cultivars) is also the most popular ornamental tree species in North America. They are grown individually or easily transplanted and moulded into thick hedges for privacy or windbreaks and they are one of the best tree species for stabilizing eroding banks or shores. They are seen as attractive because they assume such true lines and their natural tapered form appears to have been trimmed or clipped.

CHAPTER 5

THE FOREST OF ANCIENTS

They look really sort of sick and twisted…They're just ugly.
How can anything grow that slowly and still survive?[1]
Doug Larson, 1988

B y the mid-1980s, University of Guelph professor Doug Larson had carved a small career for himself as a global expert on a group of organisms known as lichens. These intriguing organisms flourish on cliffs and rock out-crops, and appear to the uninitiated as nothing more than rock scum. Even the Natural Sciences and Engineering Council (NSERC), one of the principal sources of funding for university researchers in Canada, told Doug that while his work was certainly interesting, money for lichen research was not a priority for their organization. Clearly, many others had the same opinions. Doug was one of only a handful of lichen biologists in North America.

Eventually, Doug got the hint. He decided that it was time to expand his research program to include higher plants. He didn't want to abandon lichens completely because for one, he was still fas-cinated by them, and two, he was worried that the granting agencies might cast a disparaging eye at anyone making such a radical (at least in the anal-retentive world of Canadian academia) mid-career research swing. So Doug brought in a post-doctoral student, Uta

There is a noticeable abrupt transition along the Niagara Escarpment between the cliff-edge white cedar forest and the plateau deciduous forest.

53

Matthes, a physiological ecologist and recent graduate from the Arizona State University, and Ruth Bartlett, a Commonwealth scholar from New Zealand looking to pursue her doctorate in ecology. The three of them decided that their new courses of study should be centred on a habitat with sharp ecological gradients, i.e. a habitat where the composition of plant communities shifted with distinct changes in the physical environment. They, along with prospective graduate student Steve Spring and several other researchers, ended up looking at cliffs in Muskoka that had been the focus of Doug's lichen research. Cliffs certainly had the sharp gradients they were looking for, but Muskoka was simply too far from Guelph for the type of intensive research they had envisioned.

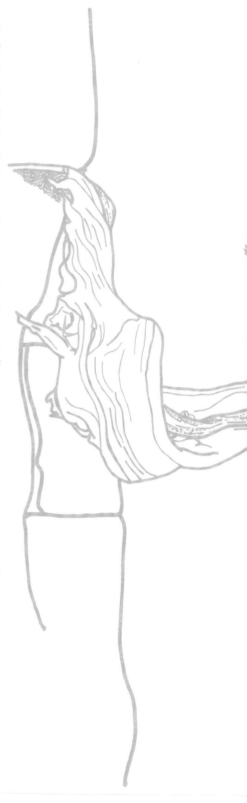

In Muskoka, Steve remarked on the unusual habit of trees growing out of rock and wondered about the physiological adaptations in these trees that would allow them to persist in a seemingly hostile environment. Steve, a rock climber, had made similar observations in the Milton area. Soon he had the rest of the group standing on the cliff edge at Rattlesnake Point, where they observed a sharp transition from a mixed deciduous forest dominated by maple in the plateau to a forest dominated by eastern white cedar at the cliff edge. What explained the pattern? Why were there no maples at the cliff edge? Had the cedars been planted? The Cliff Ecology Research Group was born. Steve went on to study the composition of the cliff-face plant community while Doug, Uta and Ruth explored the mechanisms responsible for the sharp vegetational gradient they had observed that first day at Rattlesnake Point – a pattern repeated all along the Escarpment.

By 1988 Doug had pretty well forgotten about lichens. The Cliff Ecology Research Group was in full gear. The list of potential research topics was endless as this habitat was completely unexplored. They discovered that virtually no one had conducted ecological research on the Niagara Escarpment and, in fact, very few people had conducted ecological research on cliffs *anywhere.* Every new study that yielded new answers produced even more questions about the structure and function of the cliff ecosystem.

One obvious ecological question centred on the network of hiking trails that stretched along the Niagara Escarpment cliff edge.

The group had begun to unravel the natural processes that accounted for the contrasting distribution of sugar maple and eastern white cedar at the cliff edge. But did hiking counteract these effects? Graduate student Kim Taylor had just completed her research on the impact of differing levels of hiking intensity on the composition of the plant community at the cliff edge. Doug pondered these results and wondered if hiking was influencing the ability of the cliff-edge forest (largely eastern white cedar) to replace itself. In other words, were the youngest (and therefore smallest) trees growing more slowly and therefore being eliminated from the cliff edge due to hiking pressure?

That summer, Doug agreed to supervise a high-school student named Ceddy Nash, as part of a program designed to provide students with research experience in a university setting. The hiking-impact study seemed like a logical choice. Doug and Ceddy chose two cliff-edge sites – one with a hiking trail (the disturbed site) and another without a trail (the undisturbed site) – and set out to compare the age distribution of the trees between sites. They had no inkling that the cliff-face forests might be any older than the second-growth deciduous forests that surrounded them. In fact, for years all of the members of the fledgling Cliff Ecology Research Group had assumed, like everyone else, that the cedar forest at the cliff edge was second or third growth just like all the other forests of southern Ontario!

So Doug and Ceddy innocently struck out to determine the growth rates and relative distribution of young trees to middle-aged trees to old trees. The presence of a few old trees, along with more middle-aged trees and a lot of young seedlings and saplings would be indicative of a healthy undisturbed forest ecosystem. An absence of young trees would indicate that hiking was eliminating these trees from the population. Absolute age was NOT important to the study.

Doug borrowed an increment corer to determine the tree ages. The ages would be used to calculate average growth rates. Increment corers act like biopsy needles and remove pencil-shaped wood samples that contain a record of the annual tree rings or growth layers in the tree. One ring equals one year of growth in the life of the tree. Unfortunately, it was difficult to see the rings when the cores were removed from the tree. They would need to be mounted and sanded.

On a whim, he and Ceddy cut a few small dead cedars rooted at the cliff edge. They removed a "cookie" (a cross-section of the stem) from each that could be taken back to Guelph. Again, Doug glanced at the wood but couldn't get a rough idea of the tree's age. All that could be seen on the cross-sections were saw marks. He was intrigued and took the cross-sections home to his workshop. He repeatedly sanded the wood with progressively finer sandpaper grits. First nothing, then concentric rings slowly emerged from the wood. The ring density was high and they were difficult to count. Doug held his breath and moved to a microscope. What he saw kept him awake for three straight days.

Four hundred years! Was it possible these trees were 400 hundred years old? Doug immediately thought of counter hypotheses. After all, this was his first foray into the world of dendrochronology (a science that uses annual tree rings as dating tools). He wasn't an expert. Perhaps he'd made a mistake? Trees in temperate forests were supposed to produce annual tree rings, but perhaps eastern white cedar produced a new growth layer every time it rained or there was a full moon or a bird relieved itself in its branches!? Doug's mind was racing, so he contacted dendrochronologist Ed Cook at Columbia University's Lamont-Doherty Earth Observatory in New York. Ed agreed to examine some of the samples. In the meantime, Doug and Ceddy finished the counts on the remaining samples. The oldest tree had 511 annual rings! Some of the samples were incomplete, but estimates placed the oldest tree at approximately 700 years. Ed confirmed the counts on the samples he received and yes, indeed, they were annual rings and yes, the trees were that old!

The significance of the discovery did not escape Doug. He had followed the battles to preserve the ancient white pines in the Temagami region of northeastern Ontario. This issue had mobilized thousands of protestors and lobby groups and remained a hot issue in

In this cedar tree cross-section, several decades of tree rings fit within the diameter of a penny. The hole to the right of the penny shows where decomposition started in this tree that died several hundred years ago.

Cal Clark descends the cliff face on Bear's Rump Island in Fathom Five National Marine Park near Tobermory, Ontario, during the initial 1989 survey for the ancient cedar forest along the Niagara Escarpment.

the press. The cedar he held in his hand was twice the age of the oldest white pine in Temagami. In September 1988, the results were released to the media and they made headlines in newspapers across the country. "Botanist discovers 700-year-old trees on escarpment cliffs," "700-year-old cedar trees found" and "Ancient forest discovered on Niagara Escarpment." Everyone was flabbergasted to discover that ancient trees were growing under the noses of several million people in the most densely populated region in Canada. In true self-deprecating Canadian fashion, *The Sault Ste. Marie Star* carried a small article with the headline: "Botanist erred on age of trees." The newspaper proudly proclaimed that Larson thought the trees were 40 or 50 years old but he "turned out to be wrong by a factor of more than 10"!

At the time, there was still just one known ancient tree site along the entire Niagara Escarpment: the original site where Doug and Ceddy had conducted their trampling study. The Niagara Escarpment is over 700 kilometres long. How prevalent was this forest? In 1989, Pete Kelly joined the Cliff Ecology Research to look at the age structure of this forest at nine locations along the length of the Escarpment from the Niagara Peninsula to the Bruce Peninsula. Climber Cal Clark and Pete worked their way along the Escarpment determining the ages of all trees in randomly selected transects – five-metre-wide sampling blocks that extended from the cliff edge down to the cliff/talus contact point below. The locations of transects were literally drawn out of a hat; a number in metres that would tell them how far along the cliff they should go before dropping the rope over the edge. While maximum tree age was greater at some sites than others, it became clear that the initial discoveries were not an anomaly. This study revealed that the ancient cliff-face forest was found along the entire length of the Niagara Escarpment.

The remarkable ages of these trees opened doors for other exciting research possibilities including using the long annual tree-ring records to reconstruct historical climate in southern Ontario. The success of this project not only involved the acquisition of long tree-ring records from old living trees but also a hunt for very old, dead trees; remains of previous generations that had fallen off the cliffs hundreds of years earlier. This led to remarkable finds. The initial nine-site survey by Cal and Pete had led to the discovery of an 814-year-old tree, but 935- and 1,032-year-old dead trees in the talus were discovered by Pete during subsequent surveys. In 1993, Pete explored a cliff site off the northern tip of the Bruce Peninsula that had not been visited during previous surveys. A remarkable mosaic of ancient trees lay hidden amongst the rock. This cliff supported a stunning forest of twisted trees on its face overlooking a botanical mausoleum of long-dead ancestors in its talus. Tree-ring counts from one dead tree showed that it succumbed to the elements at the age of 1,653 years! One weathered tree revealed 1,567 annual rings, but since the oldest tree rings in the wood had been lost to the elements, Pete estimated that it was close to 1,890 years in age when it died!

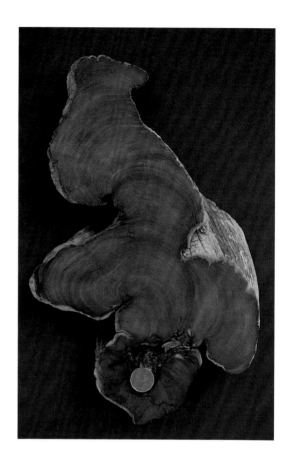

A cross-section from what may be the oldest known tree in Canada. There are 1,567 tree rings in this cross-section, but since there has been considerable erosion at the tree's base, it is estimated that this cedar was approximately 1,890 years old when it died.

This dead tree is arguably the oldest tree ever documented in Canada. The only other tree with a confirmed age rivalling this tree was a 1,693-year-old yellow-cedar (*Chamaecyparis nootkatensis*) that was cut down in a clear-cut forestry operation in British Columbia. It is not uncommon for yellow cedar, Douglas fir or western red cedar to surpass one thousand years in age in British Columbia and it is likely that many ancient trees remain undiscovered in the Pacific Northwest. We don't doubt that trees older than the oldest escarpment cedar survive in western Canada, but it is very difficult to accurately determine tree age in these species because of problems involved in trying to extract cores from trees this massive. Unfortunately, the easiest way to determine the age of a tree is to count the tree rings in a cross-section. The ages of the six oldest yellow-cedar trees in Canada (all greater than 1,300 years in age) were

Most of southern Ontario was cleared of its forests by the end of the 19th century. This circa 1885 photo of the Elora Gorge and the Irvine River Bridge shows the devastation of these early logging practices. It also shows how ancient forests could survive on cliff faces. Photo taken by William Elliott.
Courtesy of the Wellington County Archives.

all determined from clear-cut tree stumps. Many of the big trees of British Columbia are hollow, which also makes accurate age determination impossible. Yet, it is remarkable that the ages of the misshapen cliff cedars can rival or surpass the ages of these West Coast old-growth giants.

While writing and preparing this text, we wondered if anyone had taken note of the unusual cedars on the Niagara Escarpment before 1988? Even though these trees hide out on cliff faces, surely someone must have noticed their unusual morphology? Undoubtedly, some people had wondered about their unusual shape. Some may have taken the next step and surmised that they were old, but no one had gone out and tried to prove it. Would they have cared if they were old? Before the First World War, the human population thought trees were their enemy. Since they were steadfastly removing centuries-old trees from level-ground habitat for lumber or to clear the land for agriculture, it is unlikely that scraggly, old trees on cliff faces would have generated any interest. The Niagara Escarpment ancient forest is appreciated now because most other old-growth forest has been removed. Four hundred years ago when centuries-old oaks and maples were a regular component of the

Cliff-face cedars are illustrated in this engraving of the steamboat Caroline *going over Niagara Falls. Taken from* Niagara *by Ralph Greenhill and Thomas D. Mahoney, University of Toronto Press, 1965. Originally part of the J. Stewart Fleming collection, University of Toronto.*

forested landscape of southern Ontario, old trees on cliffs would have garnered considerably less interest than they do today. We have heightened their attraction to us (a collective "we") by removing everything else!

Early references to the trees were usually in the context of Niagara Falls, as much a tourist attraction then as it is now. C.A. Faxon in his 1874 *Illustrated Handbook of Travel* noted that Prospect Point on the American side was "a rough, rocky, scrubby cliff, covered with loose stones and gnarly trees, with no wall or railing even at the brink to prevent the unwary from falling over..."[2] The cliff on the American side of the Niagara River was also referenced by G.M. Grant in 1882 who referred to it as a "bold, perpendicular....cliff, almost bare, but for the scanty fringes of pines and cedars here and there [that] cling to the water-worn rifts that break its red and green and blue-black precipice."[3] Elsewhere, naturalists noted trees on Niagara Escarpment cliffs and in some cases commented on their unusual morphologies, but no one took the next step and surmised that these twisted trees might be old. In 1913, Hubert Ransier noted in the *American Fern Journal* that hart's tongue fern grew on cliffs in the Owen Sound area, but only in places "where the trees did not monopolize the space."[4] Needless to say, artists have always represented the cliff faces of the Escarpment to be places that supported only a stunted forest of cedar trees with lots of open space for such ferns.

A 1976 Ontario Parks report on the Bruce Peninsula shoreline described the cliff face as having "the usual (!) assemblage of small stunted white-cedar trees clinging to crevices."[5] The cliff was later described as "an open mosaic of depressed and stunted cedar trees with a number of hardy herbs and shrubs growing in partially protected crevices and bedrock pockets."[6] Ironically, others failed to see the trees at all. A 1963 report on important biological and natural historical features of the northern Bruce Peninsula (as prepared for a proposed national park) stated that "there is nothing botanically outstanding about the forest cover of the Bruce, at least the trees themselves…it is not the trees that are of particular interest in the Bruce but the plant communities."[7] A 1985 biological inventory at Mount Nemo described the cliff face as consisting of "a few plants such as cliff brake, bulbet fern and fragile fern with some herb robert and climbing nightshade."[8] No mention of eastern white cedars at this site even though a typical ten metre by ten metre section of cliff face at Mount Nemo supports over fifteen trees, and these trees may reach ages surpassing 850 years! Further north the cliff faces alongside the Nassagaweya Canyon were described as "sparsely vegetated consisting of a few scattered ferns and forbs"[9] in an area where we know there is ancient forest on the cliff face with cedars over 500 years old! Clearly, some people cannot see the trees for the cliff.

OTHER NORTH AMERICAN ANCIENTS

While the Niagara Escarpment is home to the oldest white cedars, it is not the only site in eastern Canada where ancient eastern white cedars have been discovered. Cedars with estimated ages up to 908 years grow on rocky islands and shorelines in the Lake Duparquet region of western Quebec while individuals up to 578 years in age have been reported from Quebec's Gaspé Peninsula. During preliminary investigations of the cliff ecosystem in Ontario's Bon Echo Provincial Park, we discovered a 910-year-old cliff-dead cedar lying at the bottom of the cliff. The potential for finding older trees here is high. Other than eastern white cedar, the only species reaching ages surpassing 500 years in eastern Canada is black spruce (*Picea mariana*). A 504-year-old black spruce was found in northern Quebec by Serge Payette at the Université Laval. Considering the extent to which the land in eastern North America was cleared of its forest cover, it is highly likely that individuals of several eastern tree species routinely surpassed 500 years in age. Unfortunately there is little evidence remaining to confirm this.

In the eastern United States, the oldest tree species is the bald cypress (*Taxodium distichum*), which grows along the rivers, streams and blackwater swamps of the southern coastal plains. In North Carolina, bald cypress trees can reach ages up to 1,622 years. Eastern red cedars over 900 years in age have been found on rocky pinnacles and steep slopes of river valleys in Missouri. Elsewhere, pitch pines (*Pinus rigida*) up to 450 years old persist along cliff edges in the Shawangunk Mountains of southeastern New York and post oaks (*Quercus stellata*) of a similar age occupy the dry upper slopes of Wedington Mountain in Arkansas. Four-hundred-year-old yellow birch (*Betula alleghaniensis*) have recently been discovered on the slopes of Wachusett Mountain in Massachusetts.

One of the most startling botanical discoveries of the 20th century, however occurred in the 1950s in the White Mountains of California. Edmund Schulman, a professor at the University of Arizona, discovered the oldest living things on earth, bristlecone pine trees (*Pinus longaeva*) over 4,000 years old growing in open canopy forests on rocky mountain slopes. A feature article in the March 1958 issue of *National Geographic* brought these trees to the world's attention. Schulman reported that these "oldest dwarves outlive the oldest giants"[10] of the American West, namely the California sequoias (*Sequoiadendron giganteum*) and redwoods (*Sequoia sempervirens*) to the south and west. These were the first trees to stretch our concept of old-growth as something more than big trees. Bristlecone pines are gnarled, twisted and stunted; their bizarre morphologies far removed from those of the towering sequoias and redwoods. Their size belies their true age. Sadly, the oldest bristlecone pine, and thus the oldest living thing on the planet, was cut down in 1964 by an overly eager young researcher who was trying to free his stuck increment borer from the tree's bole. Ironically, he was using the increment borer to determine the tree's age, made considerably easier once the tree had been cut down!

Bristlecone pines possess many of the same physical traits as the oldest cliff-face cedars, including a sharply tapered trunk, stem-stripping and a twisted and gnarled appearance.

In the past fifty years, researchers have discovered a number of very old trees from other species with similar morphologies growing in rocky habitats in the mountains of the western United States. We like to think of these species – mostly in the cypress family – as the "club of the ancients." Individual trees of Rocky Mountain bristlecone pine (*Pinus aristata*), Rocky Mountain juniper (*Juniperus scopulorum*), western juniper (*Juniperus occidentalis*), and southern foxtail pine (*Pinus balfouriana subsp. austrina*) have been found that surpass one thousand years in age including a 2,675-year-old western juniper and a 2,435-year-old Rocky Mountain bristlecone pine. The inclusion of old-growth stands of sequoias and redwoods in California would seem to give the western United States a monopoly on the world's oldest trees. Indeed, seven of the ten tree species with the longest documented life spans are found only in the western United States, while an eighth (yellow cypress – *Chamaecyparis nootkatensis*) grows in both western Canada and the United States! The only two species in this exclusive group that do not grow in the western United States are Tasmania's huon pine (*Lagarostrobus franklinii*) that reaches ages up to 2,500 years and Chile's alerce (*Fitzroya cupressoides*) that can attain ages up to 3,622 years. Alerce is second only to bristlecone pine as the oldest tree species on earth. Non-North American species with reported maximum ages approaching 1,500 years include some species of lime and fig trees, olive trees, some European oaks, the common yew, the African baobab, and some Amazonian species including the tauari or vermelho (*Cariniana micrantha*) and the Cumarú or Brazilian teak (*Dipteryx odorata*) as well as New Zealand's totara and kauri.

THE KEY TO LONGEVITY

It is probably not a coincidence that the oldest trees on earth are found in the New World. These continents were most recently settled by Europeans. Furthermore, the mountain-tops, steep valley slopes and blackwater swamps in which many of world's oldest remaining trees grow are isolated habitats. Not so for the ancient cedars. These trees grow on cliffs that criss-cross the most densely populated region of Canada. Approximately seven million people live within 100 kilometres of the Niagara Escarpment. The first ancient cedars were discovered west of Toronto, on property owned by an aggregate extraction company. This stretch of cliff is sandwiched between a large crushed gravel pit at the top of the cliff and a large open shale quarry at the base of the talus. The din of heavy machinery is ever-present at the site, occasionally drowned out by the horn of a freight train roaring nearby. Commercial jetliners sweep in low in their preparation for descent into Lester B. Pearson Airport, the busiest airport in Canada. Small planes from a local airport nearby pepper the skies throughout the day. The 401, Canada's busiest highway carries a steady stream of cars and trucks past the cliffs. Many of its bored backseat passengers are probably unaware that the green smudges on these cliffs are some of the oldest trees in Canada. The CN Tower, SkyDome and office towers of downtown Toronto are visible on a clear day. In many ways, this is *the* most unlikely spot to find an ancient forest.

Yet, here it persists. Most ancient forests tend to occur away from our most heavily developed regions. How could the ancient cedars on the Niagara Escarpment have escaped detection for so long? Well, most importantly, compared with the rest of the landscape, the cliffs were of limited economic importance. The first settlers to southern Ontario confronted the land with two clear objectives: 1) cut the trees down and sell them for lumber and 2) clear the land of trees and use it to grow crops. The cedars are the only trees to grow on the Escarpment cliffs. Back then, if anyone had noticed this unusual vertical open-canopy forest, they would have scratched their heads and dismissed it outright. Apart from access difficulties, stunted, twisted cedars weren't much use to anyone intent on making money from the forest. The cliffs aren't particularly useful for growing crops either. They're extremely difficult to plough and the costs of replacing wrecked farm equipment are excessive!

So why does an old cedar die? If left alone by humans, what is their maximum age limit? There are three possible reasons why any tree could die: 1) it is attacked by insects or fungi, 2) it is damaged by the physical environment (ie. wind, drought, fire etc.) or 3) it senesces or ages in response to hormonal changes in the tree. There is no evidence that the eastern white cedars undergo a distinct aging process. Examinations of young and old cedar trees show that age does not limit the capacity of the cambium to produce new wood. In other words, the cells in the tree that produce new cells or wood do not age. While older, slow-growing trees produced smaller tracheal cells and more latewood in their tree rings, this cell production is related to water stress and strength rather than aging. In fact, old, slow-growing trees are quite capable of producing significantly greater amounts of wood volume if they are exposed to a new or increased water supply. Many of the oldest trees (including several millennia-old intact dead trees in the talus) show no evidence of rot. The oldest tree died nearly a thousand years ago, but you could still make a bookshelf out of it today.

Death on the cliff face comes not from some pre-programmed biological change inherent to the tree but rather from forces external to it. Rockfall, storms and erosion of the cliff face are all likely harbingers of death to an old cedar. Given enough time, they all succumb to one form of natural disturbance or another. In theory, on a completely stable cliff face, protected by an invisible force field, in a climate-controlled atmosphere and tended by a legion of watering minions and fertilizing nymphs, a cedar might live for 10,000 years. However, by this point in time, even for a tree growing exceptionally slowly, the tree may become too large for its own good. Gravity may ultimately pull the tree into the talus. Unfortunately (for the cedars), none of these artificial conditions exist on natural cliff faces. The trees *are* exposed to a broad suite of harmful effects and the probability of a one-year-old cedar surviving 999 more years is roughly the same as a snail surviving a rush-hour crossing of a six-lane highway.

CHAPTER 6

NEXT STOP – THE WORLD!

I think that there is no equivalent [in France] *of your fantastic forest growing on the Niagara Escarpment.*[1]
Daniel Barthélémy, 1995

Considering that the ancient forest escaped detection on cliffs in southern Ontario, we wondered if it was possible that the same might be true elsewhere? Do cliffs around the world support an ancient forest? In 1997, Doug Larson was eligible for a sabbatical from his teaching duties at the University of Guelph. This was a perfect opportunity to investigate cliffs in other countries. Doug chose areas with climatic zones similar to that of southern Ontario, i.e. an average of 500 to 1500 millimetres of rain per year and an average annual temperature between 0° and 20° C. He narrowed his destination list down to eleven American states, plus England, Wales, France, Germany and New Zealand.

In the spring, Doug began his meanderings in the American Midwest. With help from John Gerrath, he visited exposed cliff faces throughout Illinois, Iowa and Wisconsin. Prior contact with fellow researchers in these areas had allowed Doug to assemble a list of cliff sites in each state. In Iowa and Illinois, limestone cliffs line the banks of the Mississippi. In Wisconsin, limestone cliffs outcrop near Green

Cliffs along the Danube River in Germany support ancient oaks and junipers over 300 years in age. Photo by Doug Larson.

Bay and along the western shore of Lake Michigan. Each site was visited for a few days with one goal in mind: find trees growing on cliffs and cliff edges with morphologies similar to the Escarpment cedars. Better yet, if the trees were growing close to cliff edges or to the cliff base then they could be accessed without ropes and tree cores could be readily collected. Dead cliff trees lying in the talus were especially convenient.

Iowa proved to be a good starting point. Stunted, twisted strip-bark trees were found lining the cliff edges. They resembled the eastern white cedars of the Niagara Escarpment cliffs – except that they weren't eastern white cedar at all. They were eastern red cedar (*Juniperus virginiana*), which grows everywhere along cliffs in Iowa but occupies cliff faces at just one site in southwestern Ontario. Tree cores collected from four sites revealed fifteen trees over 300 years in age. Two red cedars had 401 and 421 tree rings. The former tree is probably much older due to missing rings. A conservative estimate places its age at over 500 years. Today this is probably the oldest tree in Iowa. The oldest tree in Iowa was reportedly 448 years in age in 1975. It was also a red cedar. Although subsequent attempts to relocate this tree have proven unsuccessful, photographs taken in 1969 show its habitat. It was growing at the edge of a cliff!

The cliff juggernaut rolled through Illinois and Wisconsin. A 380-year-old eastern red cedar was found clinging to a limestone cliff in Illinois' Mississippi Palisades State Park. After one day in Wisconsin, Doug found the oldest tree in the state, and one of the oldest trees in eastern North America. An 820-year-old eastern red cedar was rooted along a cliff edge near Green Bay. Estimates made of missing tree rings indicate that it could be closer to one thousand years in age. The media in Wisconsin were amazed and the discovery made front-page news. How could a tree this old survive in the vicinity of Green Bay? Doug wasn't surprised – either at the tree's age or the media coverage. He had already seen plenty of both in Ontario. The discoveries didn't stop in the Midwest either; 469- and 473-year-old eastern red cedars were discovered on cliffs in the New River Gorge, Virginia, and a 501-year-old eastern white cedar on cliffs along the Watauga River in Tennessee.

What started as the discovery of a few old trees at one cliff near Milton, Ontario, led to our discovery of an old-growth forest along the

NEXT STOP – THE WORLD!

entire Niagara Escarpment and then to the discovery that cliffs in other parts of North America supported a similar undiscovered forest ecosystem. What about cliffs in Europe? The prognosis wasn't good. The Old World isn't a misnomer. Humans have had a profound impact on the ecology of the European continent over thousands of years, to the point that virtually nothing has been left untouched by man. After all, it was the Romans who cleared much of western Europe of its trees over two millennia ago. It's hard to believe that the endless expanses of gently rolling hills and sheep pasture of the Yorkshire Dales and the vineyards of Bordeaux were once covered with forest.

The European search began with three weeks in Germany. Doug brought Uta Matthes, his research associate and a German familiar with cliff sites in the country. Surprisingly, a quick cliff survey revealed several tree species growing on a variety of rock types. The oldest tree was a 362-year-old sessile oak (*Quercus petraea*) on a conglomerate rock face (rounded gravel embedded in a matrix of finer material) near Baden-Baden, Germany. A Scots pine (*Pinus sylvestris*) with an estimated age of 366 years was found growing on sandstone cliffs near Bad Schandau. These were important results that confirmed the idea that old trees persist on cliffs even in heavily populated areas with occupation histories dating back thousands of years.

The best was yet to come. In France, Doug, accompanied by his son Nick, headed towards the limestone cliffs of the Verdon Gorge. Doug was undeterred despite claims by French researcher Daniel Barthélemy, that there was no equivalent to the stunted forests of the Niagara Escarpment in France. Several years earlier we had come across an article on rock climbing on these cliffs in *Climbing* magazine. The photographer, while shooting the human cliff organisms, had inadvertently captured stunted and stem-stripped trees coming out of the cliff face. A photo caption referred to one of the trees being old, but apparently no one had actually bothered to determine their age. This seemed liked a logical place to start.

The cliffs towered 500 metres above the valley. From a quick reconnaissance, Doug realized that important discoveries would be made here. Spectacular examples of Phoenician juniper (*Juniperus phoenicea*) hung from ledges and cracks. Doug scouted for trees that

Doug Larson stands beside a 435-year-old juniper growing on a cliff face in southern France. Photo by Nick Larson.

could be accessed without ropes. From the top, he discovered a small number of broad ledges travelling from the cliff edge onto the face. A few cliff-face trees could be reached by crawling along these ledges. One spectacular multi-stemmed tree sat at the end of a ledge that got narrower as it got closer to the tree. Those who know Doug, know what happened next.

As Nick protested emphatically, Doug crawled along the ledge like a worm. One hundred and fifty metres up from the talus, he cut off one of the axes at its base. The tree rings were virtually invisible. After a safe retreat, several passes of sandpaper later and an extended session hunched over a microscope, Doug's suspicions were confirmed. Remarkably, the tree was 1,025 years in age! Three of the eleven other trees sampled at this site were over 300 years in age. Further north at a cliff site near the town of Chabestan, seven more samples were collected from stunted cliff trees. Here, Phoenician juniper gives way to common juniper (*Juniperus communis*) and prickly cedar (*Juniperus oxycedrus*) on the cliff faces. Five of the sampled trees were over 300 years in age including an 836-year-old prickly cedar. Daniel Barthélémy stated that he was "really happy to know that [he]... was totally wrong."

In the autumn, Doug returned to Europe to explore cliffs in England and Wales. By this time, he was expecting to find ancient

There is a striking contrast between this cliff-face forest of ancient yews in Wales and the surrounding pastoral landscape. At one time these hills would have been fully forested, as was all of the British Isles. Photo by Doug Larson.

forest on cliffs. Considering the success he had had so far, it would have been more of a surprise if he hadn't found old trees on cliffs! The Lake District and Peak District were obvious target regions for his survey. Despite a landscape dominated by rocky hills and rolling expanses of treeless pasture, Doug found clusters of dark green blotches on small rock outcrops throughout. The green belonged to English yew (*Taxus baccata*). They contrasted so sharply with the surrounding landscape, that it's amazing no one paid attention to them before, especially since they were often the only trees in sight!

While access to trees on these outcrops was relatively easy, Doug found that the English yew posed all sorts of problems. *Taxus* is extremely difficult to core because the wood is extremely hard and dense. Obtaining the tree core required strength, concentration and a barrage of foul language. The trees were often hollow or split and a large percentage of the tree rings were missing. Accurate age determination would be impossible. In the Peak District, Doug obtained up to 364 years from one tree. Considering the amount of wood missing,

A dramatic 800-year-old English yew clings to the cliff face of the Great Orme in Wales. Photo by Doug Larson.

it is likely that maximum age is twice that number. In the Lake District, maximum ring counts were 221 years with estimated ages close to 400 years. On the Great Orme in Wales, two trees yielded tree-ring counts of 372 and 469 years with estimated ages close to 700 and 800 years.

Unfortunately, old trees could not be found on cliffs in the last destination, New Zealand, although some shrub species were older than first anticipated. However, old, exceptionally slow-growing deformed trees were found growing on cliffs in the USA, England, Wales, Germany and France. The cliff trees in these countries, like the ancient cedars of the Niagara Escarpment, all share one thing in common; they appear only to those who look for them. To everyone else, the cliff and the surrounding landscape seem to overshadow the individual elements nestled within.

CHAPTER 7

THE ETERNAL OPTIMISTS

The trees composing the forest rejoice and lament with its successes and failures and carry year by year something of its story in their annual rings.[1]
Andrew Douglass, 1922

T he cliff cedars can grow so slowly that most look considerably younger than their actual age. The slowest growth that we've seen is a 430-year-old dead cedar no bigger in circumference than a silver dollar. The entire shoot weighed just 114 grams and required an average of twenty years just to add one millimetre of radial growth! Some of its annual tree rings were only one or two cells wide. In some years, the tree added no new wood and the tree ring was absent. Radiocarbon-dating was the only avenue we had for obtaining a realistic approximation of its age. In a difficult year, trees may increase their mass by less than one gram! During this time, the tree devotes its limited resources to maintaining the status quo. Like an eternal optimist, the tree concentrates on keeping itself alive until such time that conditions improve. In extreme cases like this, conditions never improve and the tree spends its entire life (albeit a long one!) on the brink of death. Of course, trees like this are exceptions, but most cliff cedars do grow slower than similar aged trees in level-ground habitats. A cedar planted in someone's yard at the turn of the twentieth

A stunted cedar less than a metre and a half in length peers out over the waters of Colpoys Bay. This cedar began life on the cliff face in 1679 A.D.

century would be a giant today compared with a cliff cedar the same age. The cliff cedar would probably be mistaken as a sapling!

Nutrient deficiency was initially thought to be a logical explanation for their stunted morphology, but an analysis of the nutrient content of cedar leaves by Uta Matthes showed no difference between cedars from several escarpment habitats. Nutrient uptake wasn't a problem either. Mycorrhizae are small root structures that are affiliated with fungi and facilitate nutrient uptake in plants. A lack of mycorrhizal fungi might negatively affect tree growth. Uta Matthes and Chris Neeser found that the percentage and density of mycorrhizal fungi was actually high in cliff and swamp habitats.

The real explanation for this suppressed growth lies within the rock. In most other cedar habitats, there is an infinite amount of rooting space. In an open field, the tree's roots have free reign to grow and expand. The only limitations to growth are imposed by the physiological limitations of the tree and from competition by neighbouring trees. Rock imposes restrictions to root expansion. There is a

The cedars reach into the cliff face, looking for any opportunity to expand their root volume.

direct relationship between the quantity of roots produced by a tree and the amount of above-ground (or above-cliff!) biomass (i.e. trunk, branches and leaves). A tiny root system cannot support a sprawling tree. In cedar, the ratio is consistent; a given mass of roots can support twice that amount in aboveground biomass.

The wide variation in growth rate amongst cliff cedars is related to the local characteristics of the rooting space for each tree and how that space changes with time. Empirical evidence suggests that the quality of rooting space has the most direct impact on cliff-face cedar growth rates, at least at the seedling stage. If the rooting space doesn't provide reasonable access to nutrients, then the cedar will be stunted relative to its level-ground cohort. As the tree increases in size, it may start to exploit fractures and cracks beyond the original germination site thus providing a previously slow-growing tree with access to new resources and accelerated growth.

Living Barber Poles

The passage of time twists, bends and curls cliff-face cedars into an infinite variety of shapes and forms. Is there another plant species that presents itself to the world in such a broad architectural spectrum? It seems unlikely. The photographs in this book should stand as evidence for this. Cedar seedlings all look the same, so the trees develop their various shapes slowly and incrementally over time. Dozens of disturbance events affect the tree during its life. The older they live the more they are exposed to natural events that alter the tree's shape, and there are as many different shapes as there are old cedars on the cliff face.

Much of the outward appearance of any old cedar is a function of the balance between its living and dead parts. The main axes or trunks of these trees are partitioned into longitudinal strips of living and dead wood. The majority of the biomass on any given old cedar is actually dead wood. While the living sapwood is bark-covered and continues to conduct water and nutrients, the dead wood is bleached white, its bark long since sloughed off. Long-dead branches cling to these whitened strips alongside the branch traces and stumps of

neighbours broken off by distant storms. Dead strips corkscrew around the stem, emerge from it and project upwards or outwards like a unicorn's tusk. The light reflecting off this white wood often provides me with the first clue that a potentially old tree is hiding amongst the cracks and hollows on the cliff face.

The strips of living wood are called strip-bark or stem-strips. On the cliff, several principal root systems may penetrate different hidden cavities within the rock. A network of extremely fine roots starts within each cavity and expands through hundreds of tiny fissures. In eastern white cedar, the strips form when one of these root systems experiences drought-induced death. During severe drought events, the water supply seeping through the rock may be interrupted. When the roots are starved of water, the conducting cells collapse and the root is incapacitated. In some tree species, such an event might jeopardize the life of the tree. In cedar and some other species (mainly conifers), the stem is partitioned into distinct bundles of conducting tissue, like garden hoses held together by an elastic band. When one "hose" is shut off, all stems, branches and associated foliage connected to it are deprived of water and die, but other hoses are unaffected and continue to conduct water. This includes the cambium, the band of cells just below the bark that triggers the formation of new wood in the tree.

In science class, did you ever insert celery into a glass of water infused with red dye? Overnight, the water moves up the celery stalk and takes on a reddish hue. If you substitute a tree root for the celery stalk, the dye will travel up the tree's trunk turning the sapwood red. Interconnections between the living water-conducting cells in the tree allow water to move around the trunk to where it's needed. This is not the case with eastern white cedar. There are direct connections between individual roots infused with dye, adjacent stem sectors (the hoses!) and branches attached to them. The dye is confined to these sectors and never penetrates the cells in the rest of the tree, even after long periods of time. This sectoring is evident in cedars as young as two years. Strip-bark formation is clearly an advantage to cliff cedars because a reduction in whole-plant performance isn't feasible amongst trees that already have exceedingly slow growth rates.

Evidence suggests that the older trees may be predisposed to these stem-strip events and they may, in fact, be essential to the continued long-term survival of the tree. There is no doubt that this internal sectoring allows the cedars to persist on the cliffs where resource availability (water, nutrients, light) is discontinuous and varied.

The extent and sequence of strip-bark events completely alters the outward appearance of each tree. A 700-year-old tree that has suffered four root death events at the ages of 50, 150, 250 and 450 years will look very different from a 700-year-old tree that has suffered two root death events at 400 and 600 years of age! Repeated root death events that affect the crown of the tree will produce a series of dead axes. The main axis dies, another assumes dominance; it dies, another assumes dominance; it dies etc. etc. The dead axes and their associated dead branches can stay attached to the tree for hundreds of years, especially if the tree is sheltered or under an overhang. Eventually, enough root death events may push it to a point where only one small root complex is all that's keeping the tree alive and clinging to the cliff face. Some of the oldest cedars find themselves in this situation. One cedar survived close to 500 years on the cliff even after 90% of the cambium (the cells that produce new wood) had died. We found a 323-year-old dead tree that lost half its cambium at the tender age of 30! Seventy-five per cent of its cambium was dead by the time it was 75 years old, but it persisted for another 250 years.

A HARD KNOCK LIFE

Of course, root death is not the only event shaping the morphology of a cliff cedar. A nasty cocktail of ill-tempered weather events batters these trees over the course of their lives. Imagine standing in the same spot for a thousand years! Wind flow towards or from behind a cliff will always generate higher wind speeds or turbulence on the face. When wind hits the cliff, there is a compression of flow as the wind is directed up and over the obstruction. You often see turkey vultures taking advantage of such winds along the Niagara Escarpment. When the wind comes from behind the cliff face, the flow separates and descends down the face creating turbulent flow.

Cliff-edge cedars are prone to storm damage especially if rot is present in the centre of the tree.

Extreme storm events, therefore, may be exaggerated in the vicinity of the cliff face and living or dead branches may be snapped off cliff cedars. Events such as freezing rain or snowstorms may have the same effect. Significant accumulations of ice or wet snow may exceed the tree's load-bearing capacity. Some cedars rooted on rock outcrops or cliffs along Georgian Bay accumulate frozen lake water during autumn and winter storms. A few trees within reach of wave action are completely stripped of branches except on their leeward side.

Gravity is also an important ecological force on cliff faces. Along with the weather, cliff cedars must contend with the constant threat of rockfall. This threat is most pronounced when temperatures hover around the freezing point. The constant freezing and thawing of water in minute fractures destabilizes the rock surface until gravitational forces pull it downwards threatening any cliff cedars (or cliff ecologists!) on its way. The Escarpment's talus slope is a testament to the large quantities of debris that has fallen off the cliffs. It has been theorized that much of this debris accumulated soon after the glaciers back-pedalled out of southern Ontario, although rock fall events of varying magnitude still occur at all cliff sites. One thousand years is a very long period of time to be rooted in an active environment and the morphologies of the oldest cedars reflect damage by falling rock. The resultant change in morphology could vary depending upon the force and direction of the impact (if the tree survives the impact at all!).

Cliff cedars, especially those along Georgian Bay, bear a remarkable load of ice and snow in the winter.

A slab of rock has fallen off this cliff, leaving only the roots of a cedar killed in the process. Some cedars may precipitate a rockfall by loosening rock as their roots expand.

Surprisingly, rock fall from above the cedar is not as important as rock fall from *below*. Let us explain. When a seed germinates on a ledge or a fissure, the roots begin to penetrate the pre-existing labyrinth of cracks in the rock. The roots establish themselves and take advantage of available pockets in the limestone. Once there, they grow and expand in volume. Roots enter through crevices then spread along vertical planes of rock parallel to the surface. Cedars only a few decades old may penetrate up to thirty centimetres into the cliff. Roots penetrate further into the cliff if the trees are not growing in soil. The roots of cedars less than forty years in age also expand an average of twenty-five vertical centimetres and over sixty horizontal centimetres along these planes. The roots may mould themselves to fit the internal structure of the rock and dense root mats are often found behind loosely attached slabs of rock. If some portion of the cliff's surface is marginally unstable, then the cracks will expand as the roots expand. Alternatively, freeze-thaw activity will hasten crack expansion. Blocks or sheets of rock separate themselves from the cliff face, the rock is dislodged and the root is exposed to the elements. It becomes dehydrated, dies and initiates a stem-strip by cutting off the water supply to part of the stem.

This process influences more than just the morphology of the tree; it can determine whether it lives or dies. If a seed lands and germinates on an unstable cliff surface with many cracks and crevices,

An army of ancient cedars clings to the cliff face at this location on Old Baldy. Note the multiple cavities created by foraging pileated woodpeckers.

the roots will have lots of room to expand. The tree will grow faster, the rock will be weakened, the rock falls and subsequent root death will occur with increasing rapidity. Unstable cliff faces support fewer eastern white cedars than stable ones. Cedars are the sixth most common plant on stable quarry walls but only the tenth most common plant on unstable quarry walls.

If a seed germinates on a solid, massive chunk of cliff face, then the roots can't expand at all, the tree grows very slowly, grinds to a halt and dies because it can't acquire the resources necessary for life. A moderately stable cliff offers the right balance between the two extremes. The seed germinates and the roots expand (albeit slowly). Rock fall and/or fluxes in water availability precipitate stem-strip formation. In an ideal situation, this will occur just as the tree is beginning to out-strip its resource base. As part of the tree dies, some of the limited resource pool on the cliff is suddenly freed for use by the newly configured cedar. If this pattern is repeated, the tree can live for many hundreds of years, living in balance with its limited resource pool.

One dead tree demonstrates this phenomenon nicely. In 1993, we discovered a breathtaking dead cedar leaning against a cliff face on an island in Georgian Bay. It sat top-down in the talus in the same position where it landed after plummeting down the cliff, sometime during or after 1082 A.D., the year that it died. This 1,700-year-old tree resembled a bag of knotted ropes. Its twisted and convoluted shape was a direct expression of the dozens of stem-strip events that shaped the tree during its life. Every time a new root cluster died, a new longitudinal strip of living bark and sapwood also died. The remaining

The remains of a 1,653-year-old dead cedar lies propped up against the side of the cliff where it died over 1,000 years ago.

living bark continued to grow and expand slowly in a fruitless effort to surround the dead wood. It isn't possible to retrace the tree's exact life history, but its growth form indicates that by the time it died, this forty-centimetre diameter tree clung upside-down from the cliff face by one solitary root. Whether the cedar became inverted early or late in its life is unclear. However, it is clear that the cliff face slowly eroded out from beneath the tree. Eventually, the original substrate disappeared completely and like a chandelier, the tree was left dangling from the cliff face. What eventually killed the tree is unknown. The roots either succumbed to the tree's weight or one final fatal drought event. Regardless, it became wedged in the talus with one solitary broken root sticking straight up in the air. Here it sat, awaiting discovery in another 910 years!

Gravity does more than send rocks and trees plummeting into the talus. Some trees are clearly affected by gravity even if they grow on a solid cliff face that shows no evidence of rock fall. Many of the cliff cedars are at least partially inverted with some of their stems, branches and crown *below* the level of the rooting point. In some cases, the rooting point is the "highest" part of the tree and the entire tree grows down toward the talus. We do not know why upside-down trees and trees with conventional growth forms can be found growing beside each other on the same cliff face. Given a choice, cliff cedars would almost certainly grow up and out from the cliff face rather than down towards the talus. Inverted trees probably started out life upright – at least for a while. Then a rock fall or nasty windstorm comes along and the tree is partially wrenched from its perch. Some roots are probably severed, part of the stem dies, and the remaining living parts of the tree get on with the business of life.

One of the more interesting morphological phenomena is the tendency for cliff-cedar branches to develop a U-shaped form, regardless of the principal orientation of the tree. They appear to grow down and away from the cliff, then readjust their position such that the branch tips point skywards. The reason for this is uncertain, but it appears that each tree and its individual parts are trying to optimize light for growth. Light is inconsistent for plants on cliff faces. It varies with latitude, season, cliff aspect (the direction the cliff faces) and time of day. Some north-facing cliffs of the Niagara Escarpment receive virtually no direct sunlight. A branch growing vertically next to the cliff face will never escape the cliff's shadow. An aspiring branch must first reach out from the cliff and then skywards to capture the most available light.

RABBITS, MOSQUITOES AND OCTOPI

An unreliable water supply, freezing rain, windstorms, rock fall, and poor light conditions all make life difficult for trees on the cliff. The magnitude, frequency and timing of these effects conspire in an infinite number of combinations to produce an infinite array of shapes and forms in the cliff-face cedars. Few cedars escape their first 200 years on the cliff without some type of damage. Just when we think we've seen all possible forms, we will encounter a cedar twisted in directions we never thought possible. As is human nature, we often assign informal labels to trees encountered in the field. Some names such as the "rabbit tree" were first applied to cross-sections collected from dead trees at the base of the cliff. The rabbit ears and the beak on the "duck tree" are stem-strips that add appendages to the forms in profile!

Other trees have been assigned ridiculous sobriquets based on their outward physical appearance. These names are usually gleaned from the natural world, such as the massive 529-year-old "mosquito tree" perched on a ledge in Mount Nemo Conservation Area. The tree appears hunched over, its stem-stripped upper axis hanging down the cliff like a giant proboscis. A large menacing eye marks the spot where a large branch broke away from the tree. The "octopus tree" is rooted near the cliff top and hangs completely upside down. This large tree is heavily stem-stripped and long, dead, white branches hang down from it like tentacles. The "waterfall tree" seems to flow or ooze down the cliff face; the curvature of the stem matching subtle indentations in the rock. The "flying elephant tree" has an elephant's head, complete with tusks, and a broken branch wing that arches skyward from the trunk. Then again, perhaps flying elephant hallucinations are what happen to a person when they spend too much time dangling off cliffs!

The 529-year-old "Mosquito Tree" at Mount Nemo.

Why Cedar? Why Cliffs?

The effect is most pronounced in spring or fall. Even from a distance, a casual observer can't help but notice the pattern. An isolated horizontal dark green band of eastern white cedar contrasts sharply with the mottled grey of limestone, in turn sandwiched between talus and plateau forests of oak, beech and maple that are either not in leaf or are aglow in autumn's reds, oranges and yellows.

In 1985, the Cliff Ecology Research Group set out to explain the contrasting pattern of eastern white cedar and deciduous forest along the Niagara Escarpment. Steve Spring's initial cliff-face plant community survey at five Escarpment sites confirmed some early suspicions. He found that eastern white cedar is clearly the most dominant tree species on the cliff face and mountain maple and the eastern red elderberry are the only other species capable of forming a canopy. White cedar abundance peaks on the cliff and plateau at or near the cliff edge and is one of the most conspicuous plants in the cliff-edge forest. Yet, the cedars completely disappear ten metres back from the

The "Waterfall Tree" flows down the cliff face at Mount Nemo.

edge where there is a sharp transition to a typical Great Lakes upland forest. Cedars that survive up to that point show suppressed growth compared with cliff-edge trees. Surprisingly, though, white cedars are very productive under conditions simulating the deciduous forest. Cedars cannot photosynthesize as effectively under the cliff-edge cedar canopy because light levels are higher in the deciduous forest. Then why are they are absent from it?

The answer has more to do with the ecological preference of sugar maple than it does with white cedar. The cliff-edge zone is more frequently stressful to plants. It experiences higher wind speeds especially in winter and spring. Soil is also shallower at the cliff edge and depleted of key plant nutrients. The shallower soil means that the cliff edge undergoes more severe wetting and drying cycles. This is very stressful to sugar maple seedlings. They respond by growing slowly. This in turn, decreases their ability to seek out soil moisture and to recover from injury. Predation of seedlings is also high at the cliff edge. Even if a maple seedling survives the periodic drought conditions at the cliff edge, it is apt to be eaten. The mortality of sugar maple seedlings after two years is virtually 100%. They cannot survive on or near the cliffs.

The cliff edge has some advantages for an aspiring plant, including a shallow litter layer. Litter is the unfortunate term used to describe the layer of decomposing plant debris (such as twigs and leaves) that accumulates on a forest floor. For eastern white cedar seedlings, a thick litter layer is lethal. In the forest, they grow more slowly than sugar maple seedlings and cannot rise above the litter to the available light. On the other hand, while the cliff edge isn't the most favourable environment for cedars, they persist here because the litter is absent and they can tolerate low light and water levels. Their smaller seeds and seedlings also provide some level of protection from predation. Cedar seedlings survive along the cliff because the maples cannot.

Cliff faces also provide one key advantage to the cedars that germinate and establish there. While new threats such as rock fall exist, the common sources of tree mortality that affect trees in a "typical" forest are absent. Competition, predators and incidences of fire are low. While competition amongst seedlings is intense in a deciduous forest, cliff cedars rarely have to compete with other plants. Even close neighbours may have root systems completely separated by rock. Predators such as small mammals do venture onto, and sometimes nest on, the cliff face but it is unlikely that they would choose to forage there given the lower plant density relative to neighbouring habitats. Fire is also not a prominent source of mortality on the face. We have only seen evidence of fire in a handful of cliff-face cedars. Any fire reaching the cliff from the plateau above, talus below or from a direct lightning strike would have difficulty spreading on the cliff face because of its open canopy.

Most tree species other than cedar also start off with a competitive disadvantage in the cliff environment. Barb Booth discovered this when she looked at the seed "rain" and seed "bank" of the cliff ecosystem. The seed rain is the total number of seeds that arrive at a given site while the seed bank is the number of seeds retained in the soil. She found that eastern white cedar seed density was very high in the seed rain and seed bank. In fact, the seed density of tree species other than cedar and white birch was very low. Barb also planted seedlings of seven tree species on artificial cliffs affectionately known as "tombstones." The experimental array looked alarmingly like a cemetery in the middle of the University of Guelph campus! Each tombstone was actually two cut blocks of quarried limestone placed on top of each other. The blocks were staggered to form small ledges. The space between the blocks simulated fissures while holes drilled into the limestone mimicked solution pockets. Growth was monitored over several years. Mortality rates were high overall yet only eastern white cedar survived the third year. Large-seeded species suffered heavy predation and four of the species were completely eliminated by the third year. Cedars also had the second most extensive root system and they were the most efficient species at allocating biomass to shoots per given area of roots. White pine seedlings grew too fast and pushed themselves out of their own planting space. Cedars kept themselves small. Cedar seedling height did not increase between their second and third year even though shoot biomass doubled.

In short, eastern white cedars live on cliffs because they can. They don't particularly like it, but a series of filters acts sequentially on the pool of species, removing one after another. Few other tree species can survive more than a few decades on the face. Given the extreme ages attained by cedars on the cliffs, all that is necessary for the perpetuation of this ancient forest is the periodic successful establishment of very small numbers of seedlings over long periods of time. If a few seedlings escape death at a young age and happen upon open rooting space within the rock, then they will survive on the face. The odds of survival may be very low for a cedar, but they're zero for all other species. An ancient forest will develop in this environment. All that is needed is time and isolation.

Cliffs and Swamps

Of course, cliffs are not the only habitats in which eastern white cedars grow. Eastern white cedars can also be found in seemingly disparate habitats such as swamps, alvars (flat rocky naturally-occurring pavements] and old fields or planted in hedges. We are often asked if the cliff cedars are the same species as white cedars in these other habitats. Yes, all of these trees are *Thuja occidentalis* or eastern white cedar. In fact, as a species, the cliff cedars aren't rare at all. Eastern white cedar is one of the most common tree species in southern Ontario. In fact, it's very likely that you or your neighbour have one growing in your yard. Of course, the cedar in your yard isn't 1,000 years old (but if it is, we want to hear about it!). It's only on cliff faces that these trees reach such remarkable ages.

The existence of "ecotypes" would explain the apparent contradiction of eastern white cedar growing in both cliff and swamp habitats. Ecotypes are subpopulations of a species that are differentiated from each other by features that are genetically "suited" for specific environments. It is thought that gene flow in any species can lead to the creation of such subpopulations. Uta Matthes looked for ecotypes

Cedars as old as 500 years also
occur on the flat limestone
pavements of the Bruce Peninsula.

in eastern white cedar along the Niagara Escarpment. She compared genetic markers known as allozymes in both cliff and swamp cedars using a technique known as electrophoresis. She found that 99% of the genetic variability in cedars was between trees in the same habitat. A stunted, gnarled cliff cedar may be more similar to a swamp cedar five kilometres away than to a neighbouring stunted cedar!

Previous studies of other tree species had found significant differences between ecotypes with regards to such factors as productivity, needle nutrient contents and gas exchange rates. Uta found no differences between eastern white cedars growing in different habitats for these same factors. Further comparisons by graduate student Chris Briand revealed similar results. An exhaustive comparison of tree architectural measurements found that there was more variation amongst cedars in the same habitat than between cedars in different habitats. There was a high degree of tree-to-tree variability. Chris concluded that individual tree orientation was primarily influenced by very local factors such as topography, wind and light. The shape and size of seeds and the number of seeds produced per cone were also compared. Again, variability was high even amongst trees within the same habitat and among cones from the same tree(!), but no relationship was found between habitats. All eastern white cedars in southern Ontario are part of a much larger homogeneous population. No ecotypes were found.

If there is no evidence of eastern white cedar ecotypes, then what physical characteristics do cliffs and swamps share that allow this species to dominate in both habitats? Firstly, cliff cedars, like their wetland counterparts, have a constant supply of water. This surprising evidence was uncovered by Uta Matthes who devised an ingenious method for artificially supplying cedars with water at an abandoned quarry site near Guelph. Discarded veterinary IV bags were cleaned and filled with water and/or nutrient solution and hung on the cliff beside eastern white cedar "patients" up to twenty-eight years in age. Trees received either a constant steady drip of water or a steady drip of nutrient solution over the course of two consecutive growing seasons. A third set of trees received nothing. Tree growth and photosynthetic response was measured carefully. The trees were then cut and the roots excavated from the dolomite. Watering had no effect on the productivity of the trees! Nutrient supply also had little effect on the trees and there was no difference between slow- and fast-growing trees. Root excavations showed that the rock was water-saturated several centimetres below the surface even during dry periods in the summer. Cedar may also be adapted to environments where a shallow rooting habit is advantageous. Cliffs and swamps would favour species with roots that spread within, rather than penetrate into the growing medium. Tipped trees in swamps and along lakeshores are unfortunate by-products of shallow root penetration.

Cliffs can be viewed as vertical swamps. While the Niagara Escarpment may appear to be a dry environment in which to live, the truth is the exact opposite. The rock is saturated with water much of the time; it's up to the roots of these trees to find it. Only extreme drought events threaten these roots (or individual root clusters). Fractured rock contains more accessible water for plants than does soil therefore the water supply to cliff-face trees may be more consistent than the supply of water to trees in level-ground habitats.

The Forest Beyond the Trees

An old-growth forest is more than just a collection of old trees. A collection of old trees isn't a viable population because it cannot replace itself. From an ecological point of view, old trees by themselves are nothing more than museum pieces or curios on a shelf. Old trees evoke powerful feelings in humans that are out of proportion to their ecological role. The true driving force of a forest, as in the human population, is the cohort of young individuals. In a "typical" old-growth forest, young trees outnumber medium-aged trees and these trees grow alongside a few very old individuals. This age distribution ensures that there are always more trees in the next youngest generation. Mortality reduces the numbers of each successive generation until the maximum life span of the species has been surpassed and the numbers drop to zero. Ironically, the trees most revered by humans are so old and so few in number that they are of little ecological importance to the forest.

Is the cliff-face forest an old-growth forest? That was the first question we set out to answer in the summer following their discovery. Selected cliff faces were sampled and the age of every tree was determined within randomly selected areas. Although there was some variance amongst sites, overall the age distribution was similar to that described for other North American single-species old-growth forests. Despite the obvious differences in appearance between the cliff-face and level-ground old-growth forests, the age structure of both forests is the same. We also determined death dates for cliff trees in the talus at one site (more on that later) and used these dead stems to reconstruct the forest population back to 1770 A.D. The age structure has remained relatively unchanged since this time. Although there have been small-scale fluctuations in mortality and germination, this is one of the few uneven-aged forests with no evidence of widespread disturbance. The density of cedars on the cliff face, as calculated at this site, is remarkably similar to level-ground Douglas fir forests in Washington, spruce forests in Sweden, and hemlock and eastern white cedar forests in Michigan.

Of course, an old-growth forest is more than just trees. Inventories of plants at several locations reveal that a consistent array of lichens, liverworts, mosses, ferns, vascular plants, trees and shrubs can be found on the Niagara Escarpment regardless of the cliff's location. Evidence collected by April Haig, a former graduate student in

the Cliff Ecology Research group, suggests that this vegetation community is consistent regardless of cliff area. Even small cliff fragments can support a vegetation community similar to that on cliff faces that extend for kilometres. The five most common vascular plants; Canada blue grass (*Poa compressa*), smooth cliff-brake (*Pellaea glabella*), bulbet bladder fern (*Cystopteris bulbifera*), common dandelion (*Taraxacum officinale*) and eastern white cedar are often seen in association with each other on the face.

We have hailed this forest as the most extensive and least disturbed old-growth forest yet described for eastern North America. Why? Because the forest is uneven-aged (healthy numbers of young and old trees), there are exceptionally old individuals, the plant community is consistent, human disturbance is generally lacking and it is almost 700 kilometres in length. Only bald cypress swamps in the southeastern United States rival the Escarpment cliff-face forest in extent and age in eastern North America.

LORDS OF THE RINGS

You don't need scientific training to determine the age of most trees. At one time or another, you have probably found yourself passing your finger over an old stump and counting its rings. It's one of the first things we learn about nature as a kid. One ring equals one year, wide rings represent good years and narrow rings represent bad years in the life of the tree. The science of using tree rings for determining tree age is known as dendrochronology (dendro = tree, chrono = time). While dendrochronology has developed into a sophisticated and multi-disciplinary science involving complex computer programs, data manipulation and statistical analyses, in essence, we have all been dendrochronologists at some points in our lives.

Believe it or not, until the twentieth century, the notion of annual rings in a tree was a poorly understood concept. Ironically, the person credited with the development of dendrochronology was an astronomer. Andrew Douglass, of the University of Arizona, was interested in sunspot activity and wondered if the variation in the width of annual growth rings in trees could be explained by the sunspot

Estimating the size of these cedars is difficult. Look at the photo above and try to estimate the size of these two stunted cedars growing on Metcalfe Rock near Red Wing, Ontario, including the 500-year-old cedar in the foreground. Now look at the photo on the right, which includes ecologist Kathryn Kuntz, to provide a sense of scale. How close were you to correctly estimating the size of the cedars? Most people overestimate the size of the cliff-face cedars.

cycle. Douglass analyzed tree-ring patterns in ponderosa pine and Douglas fir in Arizona. His efforts were moderately successful, but in the process he stumbled onto something considerably more valuable. Douglass noticed alternating sequences of wide and narrow rings in the trees. Most importantly, he realized that tree-ring patterns were repeated in different trees of the same species growing in similar environments. The death date of fallen trees could be determined by comparing their tree-ring patterns to patterns in living trees. This became known as cross-dating. The dated tree-ring sequences used for cross-dating were named tree-ring chronologies. Each new cross-dated dead tree was added to the chronology. The older the death date, the further the chronology was stretched back through time. Douglass used this procedure to cross-date beams in Native American ruins throughout the American southwest. This provided archaeologists with the precise years that trees were felled to build dwellings, and allowed them to establish when the site was occupied.

Cross-dating is the basic tenet of dendrochronology. It revolutionized archaeology, especially in Europe, as it allowed radiocarbon dating methods to be precisely dated. Dendrochronology offered the possibility of precisely dating anything made out of wood, as long as a tree-ring chronology could be developed from that species and the chronology extended far enough back through time. Researchers have used these wooden "fingerprints" to date thousands of structures in Europe from homes to castles to churches to Viking ships. Tree rings measured on the edges of wooden paintings and on Stradivarius violins have been used to confirm or refute their authenticity. Dendrochronology was even used to as evidence to convict Bruno Richard Hauptmann in the kidnapping of aviator Charles Lindbergh's baby. The tree-ring pattern on a wooden ladder left at the scene matched the tree-ring pattern in floorboards ripped up at Hauptmann's house and wood shavings in his workshop!

Tree-ring dating is also used for historical reconstructions of natural phenomena. The science of interpreting past climate from tree rings is referred to as dendroclimatology. Tree-ring width and tree-ring density are the most commonly used surrogate measures of climate. Tree rings are ideally suited for climate reconstruction because they are produced annually and each ring reflects the environment in which it was growing. Furthermore, trees of the same species in the same region tend to respond in a similar way to the incoming environmental signal. If one tree adds a narrow ring, then its neighbours will most likely do the same. Summer temperature, precipitation and drought conditions are the most commonly interpretable climatic variables from tree rings. Other natural phenomena reconstructed from tree-ring records include fire frequency, avalanche activity, glacial fluctuations and flooding. These natural events scar trees or tilt them. The event is "recorded" by the tree as a visible scar or as reaction wood; faster-growing darker wood laid down leewards of the tilt in an attempt to right itself from its newfound position.

Some species of trees are more suited for tree-ring dating than others. The rings of most tropical trees, for example, are extremely difficult to interpret and/or cross-date. There aren't distinct growing seasons in the Tropics. Other tree species don't live long enough. The cliff-face cedars, however, are ideal trees for dendrochronology. The tree rings in all but the slowest-growing trees are easily counted, measured and cross-dated. The trees have maximum life spans over a millennium and the wood is extremely resistant to decomposition. Dead trees may sit in the talus for thousands of years. The potential for long tree-ring chronologies is therefore very high. The only disadvantage to the Escarpment cedars is that they grow on vertical cliff faces! While access to the cliff edge is often difficult and manoeuvring on the face can be tricky, many of the cliffs themselves are easily accessible. Most cliffs have roads and well-travelled hiking trails within a few kilometres of, if not immediately above or below, the cliff. Cedar wood is also soft. This facilitates the use of coring equipment while dangling from a rope. If the cedars were hardwoods, it is unlikely that Pete could have completed half his fieldwork to date!

The most obvious application of tree-ring dating to the cliff cedars is in determining the actual age of the tree. Tree-ring chronologies constructed from relatively fast-growing trees can be used to verify tree-ring counts in slow-growing trees. In unfavourable years, wood is sometimes not produced by a tree in one part of the stem. If this radius is used to determine the tree's age, then the age determination may be off several years unless the tree-ring count is verified against a reliable dated chronology. In some cases, there is rot in the tree that splits the tree core into pieces. Cross-dating the broken core against a reliable chronology enables us to find out how many of the tree's annual rings have been lost to decay. Chronologies are also essential for determining death dates in cedars. In the past, this has provided us with insights into the natural mortality rates of trees in this forest. It also allows us to extend existing chronologies further back through time. Currently, a 2,767-year chronology has been developed from living trees and cross-dated dead trees in the talus.

CHAPTER 8

THE HUNT FOR CANADA'S OLDEST TREES

…very important-unbelievably old tree growing out of cliff near base.
Rappel to base and access from here. I'm not sure how I will core it.
May need monster corer. I suspect this is a thousand years old.[1]
Peter Kelly's field notes, June 24, 2003

O ur latest work is primarily a conservation effort. With funding from private foundations such as Global Forest and The Richard Ivey Foundation, and from the provincial government through Ontario Parks, we set out to conduct an inventory of the oldest trees; an initiative called the Niagara Escarpment Ancient Tree Atlas Project (NEATAP). How old are they? Where are they? Our previous research had led to the discovery of some very old dead cedars lying in the talus at the bottom of the cliff, but unfortunately, the resources were never available to permit a search for the oldest *living* trees along the Niagara Escarpment, even though previous random spatial sampling of tree ages had led to the discovery of living trees over 700 years in age. In 1995, the oldest living eastern white cedar was found during a study investigating the impact of rock climbing on the age structure, density and morphology of these trees. Two 800-year-old cedars were found in one of five random areas selected for sampling at the imposing cliff in Mount Nemo Conservation Area. Was this the oldest living tree on the cliff faces of the Niagara

This living 800-year-old cedar at Mount Nemo was found during the course of a random survey of cedars.

Escarpment? Does the maximum age of these trees vary between sites? What habitat factors contribute to longevity in this species, and will tree-ring chronologies from these trees reveal information about past episodes of climate change? Throughout the course of our research, local land managers and landowners have asked us if we know the age of the oldest tree on their properties. Some shook their head in disbelief when we told them that the antiquity of the forest as we had described it was based on "blind" or random sampling on the cliffs. We had never sought old trees! We concluded that a strategic targeted effort to locate the oldest trees at each cliff site would provide valuable information to those individuals making land use decisions along the Escarpment. After all, you can't preserve something if you don't know where it is. What does this fieldwork entail? How does one find the ancient cedars along the Niagara Escarpment? Pete takes you into the field on his quest to find the ancient trees.

A Day in the Field

Sometimes I am struck by the intense absurdity of it all. On a typical day, I can wake up in the morning, commute to my place of work within the most densely populated region of Canada and (with apologies to Gene Roddenberry) go where no one has gone before. This is possible because much of the Niagara Escarpment cliff face is still

Access to the cliff face usually involves hiking over level ground. As one approaches the edge of the cliff, it appears as a horizon line, with the darker green of the cedars announcing the presence of the ancient forest.

Peter Kelly uses an increment borer (in his left hand) to collect a core sample for determining the age of a cliff-face cedar at Rattlesnake Point.
Photo by Doug Larson.

unexplored space. For this reason, I never take a venture onto the cliff face for granted.

A typical field day begins with a selection of forgettable clothing. This is clothing that can be accidentally ripped, stained or physically destroyed, i.e. misguided Christmas presents and/or jeans with paint stains from some forgotten art project. I pick up Raj Pal, my research assistant and an extremely talented rock climber. A thirty-minute ride later and we're out of the car loaded down with equipment and heading down a footpath through a typical beech-maple forest. A telltale line of green cedar trees emerges from the mottled colours of the hardwood forest. Bright light filters through the morning haze. Similar to the way a hedge separates two properties, the cedars mark the boundary between cliff edge and open void. If you wander past this point, your next step; 30 metres straight down, will be your last. Raj perches himself on an exposed outcropping of limestone. He scatters the contents of his massive backpack on the ground to reveal a strange and colourful collection of objects more suited to the set of Star Trek than ecological fieldwork. Some items have mysterious shapes and names like grigri and jumar. Others are more recognizable including the long coils of multicoloured rope and the two-way radios. Raj uses webbing (flat lengths of interwoven nylon) and caribiners (D-shaped aluminum clips) to anchor the rope, while I put on the safety harness, tie myself in and disappear over the edge of the cliff.

Conducting inventories of old trees on vertical cliff faces can be a hazardous undertaking... but not for the reasons you might think. The most dangerous aspect of the job is not the time I spend in a harness dangling off the cliff. In fact, the time I spend on the cliff face is probably the safest part of the whole job. I am using equipment that has been lab-tested to withstand forces many times greater than the maximum forces the equipment will be required to withstand in a real-life situation. Every link in the chain between my body and the safety of the cliff top is always backed up. While I rappel down the cliff face using one rope, another person is feeding out slack on a second. Each rope is anchored by webbing (flat, finely woven ribbon-like fabric) to three points at the cliff top. The carabiners (D-shaped climbing clips) are doubled up. The rope set-up is so hyper safe that climbers routinely stop and gaze in bewilderment at the maze of rope and webbing that we have spun at the cliff top.

No, the most dangerous aspect of the job is navigating the talus; the jumble of rocks that accumulate at the base of the cliff. The talus vegetation is often a tangle of plants. Fallen logs, the dead ancestors of the cliff-face cedar forest above, are greasy when wet. The rocks themselves are often precariously balanced atop each other. Sheets of these same rocks still loom overhead on the cliff face like paleolithic

Peter Kelly stands beside this massive 643-year-old cedar that has fallen over into the talus. It may look dead, but actually it is kept alive by one tiny living branch not visible in the photo.

Above left: This large, complex 1,073 year-old cedar is rooted on the cliff face at Lion's Head.

Above right: The base of this double-trunked 941-year-old cedar, growing on the cliff in Smokey Head-White Bluff Nature Reserve on the eastern shore of the Bruce, has accumulated large numbers of loose rocks that have fallen off the cliff above.

guillotines. Carpets of jewelweed conceal the subtleties of the rocky surface below, making each blind footstep a lesson in faith. Poison ivy thrives in the rocky debris along with a number of leg-grabbing shrub and vine species. Step on the wrong rock and you will fall. Step off a rock and your leg might disappear into a yawning gap in the talus. Regrettably, the bottom of the cliff is the only place from which the cliff face can be properly surveyed. Unfortunately, walking across a slope of loose rock while gazing up at a vertical cliff face is not the easiest feat to accomplish. Throw in a pair of binoculars or a camera and the task becomes dangerous, especially when one of the old cedars emerges from around the corner.

Travelling in the talus requires concentration. On more than one occasion, just seeing an ancient cedar has sent me tumbling into the talus. I've gone around a corner, spotted a breath-takingly old, gnarled

In some cases, eroded sea caves perched high above the current water level offer protected space for cliff cedars, including this 537-year-old specimen. Its upward growth appears to have been deflected by the roof of the cave.

The roots of this gnarled 839-year-old cedar travel straight up a vertical fissure on the cliff within Lion's Head Provincial Nature Reserve.

tree on the cliff face and found myself lying amongst the rocks a few seconds later. Staring straight up while standing on a talus slope (especially if I'm staring through the binoculars) often leads to a momentary sense of vertigo and a slight imbalance. When accompanied by an ill-advised foot placement or a leg-grabbing raspberry plant, the body can careen off balance in an unexpected direction. I lunge for a flat rock. It pivots. I leap sideways onto an equally unstable rock. Then on to another. Each time, I am thrown further askew, the pack on my back adding to the imbalance. Like a talus version of hopscotch, I leap awkwardly from rock to rock desperately trying to right myself. This strategy rarely works and the game ends in typical fashion with me tumbling into a rock of unknown shape or size but of predictable hardness and density. A few scratches, a throbbing tailbone and a bruised ego, a typical albeit spectacular talus fall. Only then do I realize that this impromptu resting spot is a large patch of poison ivy.

The ancient cedars are truly awe-inspiring. It's difficult to explain why. They lack the colour of a showy flower or the flash of a tropical bird. They can't match the immense size of a coastal redwood or the power of a tornado, and they certainly don't have the "cute" factor normally reserved for some members of our native fauna. Who wants to make a fuzzy stuffed toy bearing the likeness of an ancient cedar?! Yet, they are as fascinating as a faded medieval painting or a crumbling lichen-encrusted castle that has withstood the onslaught of a thousand years of change. The oldest cedars have sat wedged in cracks for just as long, holding reign over the landscape like some forgotten monarchy. Some have witnessed radical changes to the land below. For hundreds of years, they witnessed limited land use change, an occasional fire, a clearing for a small village or field. Suddenly, there was a new commotion. The forest cover disappeared and orchards, fields, roads, quarries, subdivisions, golf courses and malls popped up in their place. Some species disappeared while others invaded the new open spaces. Some such as herb-robert, garlic mustard and the dandelion appeared beside them on the cliff face as did a few industrious humans. They are the only living things in Canada to have witnessed such change. A few trees may be older but none of them find themselves so close to human encroachment.

The industrial complex of Hamilton is visible behind the cliff face at Rock Chapel. Cedars up to 400 years in age occupy these cliffs.

So what is the "search image" for these ancient trees? Most people associate antiquity in forests with great height and massive diameter. Forests composed of such trees have been part of the public debate over conservation for many decades. Doug spent three years working in and around these cliff forests before he had any idea that the small deformed cliff trees were ancient while the large robust trees were young. This lesson was first learned by Edmund Schulman in the 1950s when he was studying the ancient asymmetrical bristlecone pines of eastern California. It was in his famous paper, "Adversity brings longevity in conifers,"[2] that he first presented the idea that plants growing slowly in extreme environments can outlive their productive cousins by several orders of magnitude.

There is a continuum of tree morphologies growing out of the cracks and crevices on the cliffs ranging from the archetypal tree, straight, vertical and lush, to smaller, gnarled and twisted individuals that may be minimal in length. The oldest trees are somewhere in the middle and even without the binoculars, they jump right out at you.

This cedar is U-shaped. The tree grows down and then back up the cliff face from the horizontal crack in which it is rooted. The tip of the tree is at the same height as its base; a situation that could only occur on cliffs!

They can be summed up by the following adjectives: deformed, stunted, gnarled, weathered, twisted, grotesque and beautiful. They bear the scars that hundreds of years of clinging to the surface of a cliff can bring. Alternating strips of living and dead wood, aborted axes, twisted stems, inverted growth form, gnarled wood, shortened internode length and a sharp taper are all characteristic of the oldest trees. Yet, no two trees are the same. Various unknown environmental factors and an unknown number of natural disturbance events over time have led to a broad diversity of morphologies in the cliff-face cedars. A relatively large and radially symmetrical cliff cedar that lacks the diagnostic morphological characteristics indicative of extreme age can be much younger than its stunted and gnarled neighbour.

After extricating myself from the poison ivy and contemplating the several weeks of scratching and scabs that await my skin, I radio Raj; he tags the cliff-edge location above the tree and I head back up top. Raj works his magic and finishes setting up the ropes. Since Raj can't see the tree, it is important to accurately tag a location immediately above it. If I'm off-target, and I cannot reach the tree, I will have to return to the cliff top and Raj will have to reconfigure the ropes. I struggle with my harness and wonder out loud why any male voluntarily places himself in such a restrictive apparatus. I attach a locking rappel device known as a "grigri" to one line and attach the grigri to my harness. This device will control my descent. Raj will control a back-up belay line that he now ties into his harness. This is the safety line. If some unforeseen event incapacitates me or the rappel line, Raj will be able to assume control of my descent. There can be no accidents.

I now start gathering all the equipment I will need on the cliff face. I do not want to forget anything! Most importantly, I grab my helmet then I attach the genuine naugahide increment borer carrying case (where do naugas come from anyway?) onto my harness. Very little of the genuine naugahide can be seen anymore. It didn't stand up to the wear and tear of the cliff, so it is now a long glistening beacon of duct tape. Next in line is the dull green "Made in China" shoulder bag that contains my field notebook, along with pens, markers, spare batteries, aluminum tags, wire, clippers, tape measure, Zip-loc bags, straws, masking tape and hundreds of fragments of leaves, twigs and branches that have worked their way into the bag over the course of the field season. I offset the weight of the corers hanging off my left side with the weight of the green bag on my right. Since I need space in front of me to work the ropes, I will use a carabiner to attach the large brilliant orange Pelican carrying case that holds my camera equipment onto the metal ring above my butt at the back of the harness. Next, of course, is the golf ball retriever. Excuse me? Yes, believe it or not, the golf ball retriever has become an integral part of our field gear. We paint the extended retriever in ten centimetre increments. It is perfect for measuring out or up from any position on the face. The golf ball retriever goes over my shoulder using a strap made from webbing and attached with duct tape (of course!). Last but not least, I hang my two-way radio from my belt. I've got so much stuff hanging from me, I feel about as balanced and mobile as a drunken sloth.

If I have ever had a fear of heights, I have long since lost it. This is a bad thing. I have always regarded a fear of heights as a rather healthy phobia even though it might seriously hamper my ability to pursue ecological research on cliffs. You might think that the genes that propel humans into stepping off perfectly solid cliff tops would have been selected against and filtered out of the population a long

time ago. Not surprisingly, I have discovered that this danger to
humans is one of the factors that has protected these trees long after
their level-ground brethren were turned into furniture and paper.

Despite this lack of fear, the first step over the edge is always the
most awkward. With my back to the open abyss, I press my feet firmly
against the rock and slowly lean backwards in an attempt to align my
body perpendicular to the face. If my feet slip, I'll swing into the rock
(and my feet have slipped – many times). At the earliest opportunity I
stretch out and peer straight down. I'm checking my position against
the location of the tree base to ensure that the two are aligned. I'm
also anxious to get my first close-up glance at this tree.

It's a magnificent specimen that is rooted on a small ledge no
bigger than a foot stool. Its roots disappear into a series of ominous
vertical cracks in the rock at the back of the ledge. There is no soil to
speak of, except for a thin layer of dark organic matter that has fallen
from above and accumulated at the back of the tree. The tree extends
several metres straight out from the cliff face before ending at the
stunted dead tip of the original growth axis. Two distinct strips of
living bark-covered conducting tissue snake their way up the trunk
beside the bleak whitened expanses of dead wood. Before the end
they take a right turn downwards. From here they meander their way
five metres along the new living axis of the tree (and former branch).
Each of the living strips (punctuated by a series of emergent dead
branches) culminates in two distinct clusters of sparse green foliage.
It's hard to believe that the two clusters of leaves that dangle many
metres below its base are in fact the tree's canopy.

Nearby, a number of younger cedars are perched like pupils
gathered around their mentor. I am forced to endure jabs from their
branches just so I can access the root base of the target tree. Once I'm
comfortable and secured on the face, Raj will use a Global Positioning
System to accurately record the tree's longitude and latitude. I record
a number of very specfic site variables including the dimensions of
the rooting point, the presence and size of overhangs, the direction
the cliff is facing and an assessment of rock stability. Raj lowers an old
climbing rope marked in one-metre increments, which we use to
measure cliff height, distance from tree base to cliff edge, and from

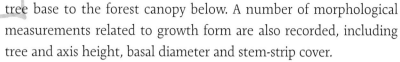

tree base to the forest canopy below. A number of morphological measurements related to growth form are also recorded, including tree and axis height, basal diameter and stem-strip cover.

The age of the tree is determined with a handheld hollow coring device known as an increment borer. Like a biopsy needle, the borer is used to collect a thin 4-millimetre-wide piece of wood from the tree containing a lifetime record of annual tree rings. Unfortunately, while an increment borer is a relatively straightforward tool to use on level ground, it creates a whole series of problems on the cliff face. Newton's First Law of Motion states that every body will continue in its state of rest unless propelled by "impressed forces." In other words, an increment borer cannot be drilled into a tree if the user is dangling in mid-air and unable to apply an 'impressed force' in the first place! To rectify this deficiency in force I often have to wrap my legs around the tree or attempt to core with one arm while the other is desperately hanging on to the cliff face. This position gives new meaning to the concept of tree-hugging. Sometimes it's not possible to core the tree near its base because the adjacent rock interferes with any attempt to turn the handle on the borer. It was also Newton who discovered the principle behind the fact that pens, field books, camera lenses and parts of increment borers will travel downwards rapidly when dropped from a cliff face.

I retrieve the tree core from the shaft of the borer using a long thin metallic U-shaped strip known as a sleeve or spoon. With one hand gripping the tree for balance, my other hand inserts the spoon into the borer where sharp teeth grip the tree core. Ideally, the core is then pulled from the borer with my third hand and stored for future analysis. Not surprisingly, since I (and most other humans) lack a third hand, I sometimes lose the core at this stage as it emerges from the borer. A slight shift in balance or a sudden updraft (it's often windy on the face) and the core will blow free of its resting spot and perform an intricate ballet as it drifts into the dense vegetation of the talus below. If I manage to retrieve the core, I place it in a plastic straw and seal it until it can be safely extracted and mounted. I have discovered that the Mcstraws available in a certain unnamed mega fast-food chain are the perfect size for tree core storage.

A turkey vulture chick in its rock nest on a cliff face within Rattlesnake Point Conservation Area.

I finish up at the tree and tie a labelled metal tag to it. With the feeling gone from my legs, I descend towards the talus below. Hssssssssssttt! I stall my descent. Hssssssssstttttt!!! I hear an intense and persistent hissing that sounds like radio static coming from a crevice cave halfway up the cliff. Cliff faces provide habitat for a number of mammals, songbirds, insects and microorganisms, but I cannot think of a creature that makes a sound like this! While balanced on a small ledge, I peer into a dark void. A fetid stench drifts my way. A slight movement at the back of the cave and the sudden appearance of a looming shadow on the cliff face confirm that I have stumbled upon a turkey vulture nest. Within a couple of seconds, the chick, beautifully displayed in black and white down feathers, reveals itself and musters up another extended gut-wrenching hiss. I recall vague memories about the remarkable vomit-hurling capabilities of turkey vultures in distress. A quick recall of their diet and I beat a hasty retreat to the talus. I release myself from the ropes, loosen the harness and collapse onto the rocks. The feeling must return to my legs before I can make the trip back up to the cliff top.

The following day, the samples are removed from the straws and carefully glued into wooden mounts. A drill press with sanding head is used to reduce the rough surface of the cores to a smooth polish. Under a stereomicroscope, I count 581 rings in the first core.

This core includes the pith (or first year of the tree's growth) but ends with an outer ring that died an unknown number of years ago. I repeat the process with a different core that missed the pith but contained the current year's growth as the outer ring. This sample contains 612 tree rings. Clearly, however, the tree is actually much older. The individual tree-ring widths are measured and a cross-dating program is used to match the patterns of variation in tree-ring widths between the two cores. The dead portion of the tree died in 1842, thus establishing the germination date as 1261 A.D., almost 740 years in age. An important tree, no doubt, but only one of the many ancient trees left to be discovered on the cliffs of the Niagara Escarpment.

CHAPTER 9

CLOSE ENCOUNTERS

For hundreds – in some places, a thousand or more – years, nothing has been cut, no roadways have been cleared. There has been growth and death and rebirth, but those occurrences are all so interconnected it would be difficult to distinguish one from the other.[1]

Barry Stutz, 1993

I n the last five years, we have sampled nearly 600 living trees at various locations along the 735 kilometres of the Niagara Escarpment, and close to 250 of these trees have turned out to be exceptionally old for their respective cliffs. Ten of these cedars were found to be over 1,000 years old! Two cedars began life as seedlings over 1,300 years ago. You can imagine how different the world was back then compared to what it is today.

The ancient forests of the Niagara Escarpment are an important component of our diminishing natural heritage. Land-use policies cannot be implemented to ensure their protection if the significance of the resource is not fully realized. We hope that future generations at the turn of the next millennium will be able to hike along the Niagara Escarpment and observe some of these same trees. Hopefully they will take comfort from them. I hope you do the same. The following pages will provide you with a rare glimpse and stories behind twelve of these spectacular trees.

This is the second oldest living eastern white cedar. It germinated over 1,300 years ago in 701 A.D.

| The ten oldest living cliff-face cedars found along the Niagara Escarpment. | | | |
Age in 2007	First Year	Height (m)	Diameter (cm)
1,320	688 A.D.	6.9	69
1,307	701 A.D.	8.0	65
1,217	791 A.D.	5.6	62
1,213	795 A.D.	4.5	22
1.160	848 A.D.	8.7	69
1,148	860 A.D.	6.8	69
1,074	934 A.D.	7.5	57
1,056	952 A.D.	2.4	39
1,037	971 A.D.	10.5	75
1,010	998 A.D.	4.7	41

The Ghost

> Location: Beamer Memorial Conservation Area,
> Grimsby
> Basal Diameter: 32.4 centimetres
> Height (Living): 7.3 metres
> Cliff Height: 3.8 metres
> Date of Birth: 1787 A.D.
> Age in 2007: 221 years

Sometimes the most interesting trees aren't necessarily the oldest. I discovered this tree during the first inventory of cliff cedars in 1989, but did not sample it. At that time, my concerns were centred on living trees only. We wanted to know if the cedar trees were part of an undisturbed and self-sustaining old-growth forest. Sections of cliff face were randomly selected (cliff sections were literally chosen by drawing numbers of a hat!) and we determined the ages of all living trees within those sections. This tree was not in one of the selected

The Ghost, discovered within Beamer Memorial Conservation Area: date of birth, 1787 A.D.

areas. Still, I was fascinated by it. Its inverted and gnarled trunk gave it an otherworldly appearance. I photographed it but never examined it closely.

In 1998, as part of the Niagara Escarpment Ancient Tree Atlas Project, I returned to this site to find the oldest cliff cedars. I was hesitant because the talus is hell. The cliff face is actively eroding at its base and the talus below is extremely steep and unstable. The face is severely overhung by a more resistant caprock that is perched menacingly overhead. Most of the cedars are rooted near the top of the cliff on the more stable rock. Unfortunately, I could not get a good look at the trees without venturing out onto the mobile talus slope. On several occasions I found myself sliding downslope out-of-control through large patches of poison ivy. The resultant blisters were mementos of these cliffs for weeks to come!

Nine years on from my first encounter with this tree, I was amazed to discover that it hadn't fallen into the talus; a seemingly impossible feat for a dead tree hanging upside-down off the edge of a cliff. I became suspicious and was amazed to discover that the tree was actually alive! A living root anchors the tree on a small ledge nearly a metre down from the cliff face. The living bark strip is concealed at the back of the tree and culminates in one living branch that descends towards the talus before arcing skywards. I had missed the scant living foliage because it blends in with the surrounding talus vegetation.

It is only 221 years old (only... it began life before the French Revolution!) but it is a testament to the tenacity of eastern white cedar. It moves back and forth with a gentle push not unlike the quintessential hanging log that guards one hole on every miniature golf course. The trunk is hollow near its base and the one living branch produces a quantity of foliage on par with a large houseplant. Yet it has endured in that position for over a decade and probably much longer. Who knows how long it can persist on the cliff face? There is no reason to think that in fifty years time when many of its level-ground neighbours have come and gone, that it still won't be hanging off the cliff face, gently swaying in the breeze.

THE CLIFF GIANT

> Location: Crawford Lake Conservation Area, Halton
> Basal Diameter: 69.0 centimetres
> Height (Living): 12.8 metres
> Cliff Height: 6.6 metres
> Date of Birth: 1717 A.D.
> Age in 2007: 291 years

Crawford Lake Conservation Area is an extremely popular destination. A pre-historic Iroquoian settlement has been reconstructed in its original location in the plateau back from the cliff edge. A hike through the vast tract of second-growth hardwood forest in the plateau will bring you out to the cliff edge with a spectacular view of Buffalo Crag and the Nassagaweya Canyon. The base of the cliff, however, is difficult to access and it receives little traffic. Some parts of the talus are so thick with vegetation that traversing the base of the cliff is a challenge. Walking gives way to scrambling and, at times, crawling. On a hot, damp summer day, it feels like a small chunk of rain forest got lost on its way through southern Ontario. Catching sight of this cedar on the cliff face makes the experience even more surreal.

It is massive. It is the largest eastern white cedar to be discovered on the cliff faces of the Niagara Escarpment. One other cliff-face cedar is bigger in diameter and a few are taller, but no others come close to it in sheer mass. It is the antithesis of everything you've just learned about the ancient cedars. It is by no means stunted (although it may still be smaller than 291-year-old cedars in other habitats!).

The Cliff Giant, discovered within Crawford Lake Conservation Area: date of birth, 1717 A.D.

Rapid radial growth during its life has produced tree rings several magnitudes bigger than a typical cliff cedar. It grows straight up the cliff face and only a tiny portion of the cambium is dead. Unlike other cliff cedars, most of the conducting tissue is still living in this tree. The only morphological traits that it has in common with other cliff cedars is the spiral growth pattern in the top half of the tree and a main axis that has been snapped off in a storm. Otherwise, you would never know that this tree grows on a cliff.

At first glance, it seems that the tree isn't attached to the cliff face. Close to a tonne of wood and bark seem to float in mid-air almost four metres above the base of the cliff. Once I actually got on the ropes and descended down to it, I discovered that the tree began life on a ledge approximately five metres long and only half-a-metre wide. The roots are anchored in a horizontal crack but are attached to the tree below the rooting point. Another root exits the tree a metre above its base to provide a second anchor point on the face. This may provide enough stability to the tree to keep it from succumbing to wind or gravity.

Why it grows so fast is a mystery, but the secret undoubtedly lies within the rock. It may have access to an unprecedented supply of nutrients and water and may actually be tapping into a spring within the rock. Clearly, 291 years ago, the seed that gave rise to this tree happened upon an ideal spot for growth. Unfortunately, its sheer size makes it extremely susceptible to the forces of gravity, and every year that it lives, it becomes more vulnerable. If it continues to grow at this rate, at some point in the relatively near future, its weight will surpass the ability of the roots and cliff to support it. Long after it has fallen into the talus, its older but smaller neighbours above it will continue to flourish on the face.

THE MILLENNIUM TREE

> Location: Lion's Head Provincial Nature Reserve
> Basal Diameter: 38.8 centimetres
> Height (Living): 1.65 metres
> Cliff Height: 24.5 metres
> Date of Birth: 952 A.D.
> Age in 2007: 1,056 years

In general, surveying for old trees along this cliff was relatively easy. Yes, the talus was a harrowing collection of mobile sheets of rock, fallen trees, dense shrubbery and poison ivy, but once I found a stable position at the bottom of the cliff and gazed upwards, the trees stood out like graffiti on a wall. Most of the oldest trees have set roots on the hard dolomitic caprock in the upper half of the cliff. Few trees have successfully colonized the severely undercut lower half. The bedrock here peels off in a plane parallel to the cliff face. This is not only dangerous for anyone venturing along the cliff bottom, but it makes life difficult for trees with great aspirations of longevity.

But none of this, of course, explains why a one-thousand-year-old tree was found living on a ledge on this cliff. Let me explain. As I was stumbling along the bottom and surveying the cliff face for potential old trees, I came upon a peninsula of rock projecting out from the face. I travelled around this outcrop several times craning my neck to see what was on top. I spied an exceptionally old-looking dead cedar, but I could not tell if there were any old living trees as well. I noticed a few sprigs of green foliage blowing about in the wind, but the tree itself was remarkably hidden from view, as though it didn't want to be found. I hummed and hawed, but finally decided to mark this spot and rappel down to it from the cliff top along with other previously marked trees. For all I knew it was a straight, vertically unchallenged 30-year-old tree, but I didn't want to leave any stone unturned (so to speak!). I took some notes,

The Millennium Tree, discovered within Lion's Head Provincial Nature Reserve: date of birth, 952 A.D.

continued the survey and immediately forgot about that spot, my thoughts now absorbed by the spectacular cedar on the cliff in front of me.

Weeks later, I sat perched at the cliff edge above this spot. We were working our way along the cliff edge, and I was rappelling down the face to trees previously earmarked for sampling. Comments I had written in my notes jogged my memory about the unusual outcropping and the cedar on top (that I had never seen). Not likely to be much, I thought. I squeezed into my climbing harness, attached myself to the rope and walked down to the face to the edge of the overhang. Below this point, I would be hanging suspended in mid-air, close to eight metres separating me from the cliff face under the overhang. I manoeuvred my legs into open space, released the handle on the grigri and slipped into the abyss.

Now I had my first glance at the tree that had eluded me weeks earlier. I stopped breathing. It was spectacular! This was no 30-year-old sapling. I tried to absorb its subtleties, but the rope was twisted and it had me spinning in tight circles above the ground. As I had no way of alleviating the situation, my impressions came as quick observations and quick glances over my shoulder as I spun away from the cliff face. The base of the tree was thick and contorted. Its height was only four times its diameter! Several large sheets of rock were perched above it and several rested atop its base. It was difficult to see, but the only living bark-strip emerged from the rock on its underside. I knew instantly that this tree was something special and even without extracting a core I knew that it couldn't be less than 500 years old.

This begged the question: How was I going to take a core from this cedar? How was I going to get myself close to it? I was dangling in mid-air many metres from the cliff face. Below me, I could only see treetops. Since I had nothing to push against, I wasn't moving eight centimetres closer to the cliff face let alone eight metres. The only logical albeit difficult route was to descend into the talus cedars, push against one of them, pendulum over to the outcrop, then climb up to the tree from there. The plan worked well except for a few small details. As I did my best Tarzan impersonation and swung over to the rock, I had only a second to find a suitable handhold to grab onto. At the same time, I had to release the tension on the rope that was trying to pull me back off the rock face. Many attempts and a few scratches later, I found myself clinging to the face.

Looking up, I could see that the rock was terraced and several small faces blocked my access to the tree. While these weren't difficult to climb, it did involve scrambling over precariously balanced razor-sharp, vertical slabs of rock. Every step upwards involved a mental risk assessment and a careful evaluation of the forces being exerted upon each slab of rock. When I finally unceremoniously plopped myself down beside the cedar, I couldn't begrudge its choice of home. If one had to spend a thousand years in one spot, one could do much worse than this rocky spot with its stunning view of Georgian Bay's clear turquoise waters and the cliffs that skirt its shores.

I didn't know it at the time, but this hidden and inaccessible tree was also the first living millennium-aged tree that I had found. Ironically, I wouldn't know its true age until months later after the cold and blowing snow had rendered fieldwork impossible. Sometime in February, when winter had long since descended upon the Escarpment cliffs, I stared at the tree core under the microscope. I marked ten-year, fifty-year and hundred-year increments with dots. Dozens of dots passed through the field of view before I reached the end of the core. Only then, did I realize that how close I had come to not discovering it at all.

A cluster of five ancient cedars within the Inglis Falls Conservation Area south of Owen Sound, including one tree we called the Bowsprit that runs diagonally in this photo from upper right to lower left: date of birth, 1390 A.D.

THE BOWSPRIT

Location: Inglis Falls Conservation Area
Basal Diameter: 39.6 centimetres
Height (Living): 7.7 metres
Cliff Height: 13.2 metres
Date of Birth: 1390 A.D.
Age in 2007: 618 years

Grey Sauble Conservation Authority approached me about including a recently acquired property of theirs in the Niagara Escarpment Ancient Tree Atlas Project. They were interested in opening up the site to visitors and wanted to know if there were cliff sites more prone to disturbance and human traffic than others. I travelled to the site one morning in the spring and met with members of the GSCA to get my first look at the site. I saw some interesting cedars on the face, but nothing that appeared over 300 years in age. I was happy to include the site in my inventory, but I wasn't expecting to find anything earth-shattering. When we returned here in the summertime to conduct an inventory of the face, I came across one area that I hadn't noticed first time around. Five very old-looking trees were crowded together along one short section of cliff edge, a horizontal distance of less than five metres. Another clung to the face another five metres away.

I was shocked to find that this small area was home to a number of old trees. In fact, there may be no other spot along the Niagara Escarpment with this concentration of ancient cedars. IFI-692 is the oldest of the lot. It germinated in 1390 A.D.; and is over 610 years in age! The ages of four others ranged between 450 and 500 years! The sixth was 337 years old. These ages are unusual because the trees are growing at or just below the cliff edge and most are accessible to unwanted visitors, including the loggers who cleared the forest at the cliff top. Luckily this group of trees escaped unscathed except for one cedar with several cut branches.

There is no obvious reason why six trees growing so close to each other would have survived for over three centuries. Perhaps they are naturally sheltered from the wind? Regardless, even at the close of the 17th century, these six trees were already here, albeit smaller in size. IFD-692 was already 300 years old at this point! It would be interesting to travel back through time and see the orientation of this tree then. It is difficult to imagine how its morphology evolved through time. In its current orientation it seems to defy gravity. It projects straight out from the cliff face like the bowsprit on some great sailing ship. Even the upper surface is dead, the bark having sloughed off to expose wood bleached and eroded by the elements. Because of rot near its base, I was forced to shimmy along the trunk to obtain a solid tree core. I couldn't help but feel like I was walking the gangplank!

One its neighbours posed an interesting problem for working at this site. A hive of bees had made their home inside IFI-694 and became agitated every time I approached the trees. In fact, while fieldwork at this site was completed in July, I had to return at the end of October to core IFI-694 when bees' activity was sufficiently slowed down by the cooler weather!

THE AMPUTEE

Location: Mount Nemo Conservation Area
Basal Diameter: 47.3 centimetres
Height (Living): 4.3 metres
Cliff Height: 29.5 metres
Date of Birth: 1134 A.D.
Age in 2007: 874 years

In 1134 A.D., a small cedar seed blew onto this ledge overlooking the undisturbed verdant forests of southern Ontario. The seed germinated. A tiny plant absorbed its first rays of sunshine. The Inca Empire was about to be born, the First Crusade had just led to the storming of Jerusalem and Genghis Khan was still a twinkle in his parents' eyes. The Niagara Escarpment didn't exist as a place name. No one cared whether this tiny seedling lived or died. A year went by and most of its cohort died, shrivelled up and blew away. Another winter, another summer, another winter and our seedling continued to eke out a life on this rocky face.

For over six hundred years, while much of the rest of planet was undergoing the ebbs and flows of the human tide, this cedar persisted and flourished in its rocky hideway. Then, humans took hold of the surrounding landscape. Within 200 years, virtually everything had been altered by the human tidal wave *except* the narrow expanse of vertical bedrock it called home. However, odds were good that this expansion would go no further. Cliffs provide an effective barrier to bipedal organisms. Or do they? After 820 years, you would think that an immobile organism like a tree would have seen everything. But, it's not true. Against all odds, humans started appearing on the face. Eventually they even shared the same small ledge space. The last frontier of human expansion had been broken.

I first discovered this tree in 1995 while conducting research on the impact of rock climbing on the cliff-face cedar forest. This now lopsided tree occupies a ledge halfway down a thirty-metre cliff face in Mount Nemo Conservation Area. A climbing route known as Devil's Staircase dodges the north side of the tree while a thirteen-metre

Detailed drawing of The Amputee, showing that various branches have been sawn off.

*The Amputee,
discovered within
Mount Nemo
Conservation
Area: date of
birth, 1134 A.D.*

The Alien, discovered within Fathom Five National Marine Park at Tobermory: date of birth, 1179 A.D.

unclimbed section of cliff abuts it to the south. Yes, those are saw marks! Every branch on the north side of the tree has been cut off, as if a giant had made a swipe at it with an oversized chainsaw. Eighteen cut branches were removed from the tree on this side, at least two of which were living at the time. By comparing the pattern of tree-ring growth in these cut branches with tree-ring growth patterns in the main stem, it was revealed the damage took place in 1992 and/or 1993. Other trees have also been completely removed or damaged in the area, including a tree sawn off at its base. The tree is kept alive by two living branches on its south side that support several clumps of living foliage.

This tree is symbolic of all issues related to human pressures on natural ecosystems. Few people would disagree that ancient trees such as MNN-681 merit protection, especially in the heavily altered landscape of eastern North America. While many may argue for or against the merits of rock climbing, the reality is that thousands of people within driving distance of the Niagara Escarpment are avid rock climbers. These people need access to the climbing resource but not at the expense of the oldest and most extensive old-growth forest in eastern Canada. This is the dilemma facing landowners, policymakers and the rock-climbing community. Concessions on all sides of the issue will be necessary if we agree that future generations of Canadians would appreciate this forest as much as we do now. If we could live 200 years in the future, would we be happy that our ancestors lacked the foresight to protect trees up to a thousand years old? Would we be happy knowing that the bare cliffs of the Niagara Escarpment once nurtured an ancient cedar forest? I think not.

THE ALIEN

> Location: Flowerpot Island, Bruce Peninsula National Park
> Basal Diameter: 44.4 centimetres
> Height (Living): 3.7 metres
> Cliff Height: 15.8 metres
> Date of Birth: 1179 A.D.
> Age in 2007: 829 years

"Welcome to Flowerpot Island...that orange stuff on the rock is a plant called lichen which lives on the cliffs. Over there on the cliff you'll see the profile of a woman. She's an Indian princess who..." I've probably heard the same spiel a hundred times. Flowerpot Island is one of the most popular destinations in Bruce Peninsula National Park and every year thousands of people take the tour boats from the mainland to see the two unusual rock formations popularly known as The Flowerpots. What few people on those boats realize, including the tour operators, is that the most interesting feature of that cliff face is not the lichen or the fabricated story of the princess "frozen" in the rock, but the oldest trees in eastern North America – one of which has lived on the cliff for over 800 years.

FPS-733 may be the most noticeable ancient cedar on the Niagara Escarpment. It is easily visible to the tour boats plying the waters off Flowerpot Island and every summer day, thousands of people float past it on their way to the island's docks. It is a prominent feature of the cliff on the island's south side. I have wanted to know the age of this tree since first seeing it from a boat while heading to the island to conduct fieldwork in 1990. Unfortunately, my priorities have always lain elsewhere. In 1999, I had my opportunity when I included Flowerpot Island in the Niagara Escarpment Ancient Tree Atlas Project.

It seemed a perfectly legitimate plan at the time, but I didn't anticipate the unique problems associated with doing fieldwork on this cliff face. Apart from the obvious logistical problems associated with living on an island, our first challenging problem was to actually find a navigable route to the cliff top – our only means of reaching the trees on the face. The oldest trees occupy a cliff face on South Bluff, a mesa surrounded by cliff in all directions except to the west where the cliff is broken down into a series of short outcrops and massive limestone boulders. Unfortunately, this was not a practical route as we were staying in an old ranger cabin east of the cliff site. We needed to find a route that we could access with relative ease several times a day. Eventually, we found a sketchy route up the east face that, while not ideal, was our only real choice.

Unfortunately, the forest on the cliff top turned out to be a barely penetrable hodgepodge of fallen trees, logs, and dense clusters of eye-poking hemlock, spruce and cedar trees. The cliff edge was even worse. Rather than a distinct cliff edge, the top gradually sloped to the cliff face. An extremely dense forest of eastern white cedars occupied this slope. So dense, in fact, that it could take me, with my gear and ropes, up to ten minutes to squeeze through the ten metres of tightly packed stems. I had to work my way around each tree individually, sometimes removing all my gear just to navigate around one tree. Almost every location was the same. This obstacle alone made it more worthwhile for me to walk around the cliff and back up our access point then to climb back up the face. The lack of trails or evidence of humans was a welcome change from most other cliff sites, but it also made fieldwork very difficult. FPS-733 also posed another problem. This cedar was growing under an overhang. I had to rappel down beside it, shimmy my way along the face, grab onto the tree and pull myself under the overhang.

I had been concentrating so hard on the task of actually reaching the tree that I had failed to pay much attention to it – until now. What extraterrestrial race arrived on earth and left one of its citizens behind on our cliff face? This cedar is truly bizarre looking. Up close, it is menacing. It rears up and lashes out from its cave like some alien creature disturbed from its sleep. Its gnarled and contorted trunk gives rise to a myriad of bleached and gnarled dead branches; appendages grasping for some imaginary prey. It is beautiful, yet grotesque at the same time. No other cliff-face cedar demonstrates the power of time more clearly than FPS-733.

Despite the monumental effort required to reach this tree, I still wasn't sure that this it was even alive! Clearly, the main axis was dead but was the cluster of green foliage nearby connected to it or part of a separate individual? The base of the tree was littered with rocks that had peeled off the roof of the overhang, concealing the base of the living branch (tree?). I removed several of these and, yes, the two were connected. The tree was still alive. Subsequent cross-dating of the tree rings in both living and dead axes indicated that the tree began life as a very ordinary looking seedling on or about the year 1179 A.D. The branch that gives rise to the only living foliage present on the tree appeared around 1321 A.D. when the original stem was approximately 140 years old. Unfortunately, for unknown reasons most of the tree gave up the ghost in 1849. The entire main axis died except for one living branch exiting the tree near its base.

On this cliff face, this cedar was a welcome relief from most of the others because the overhang provided some degree of shade. This cliff faces due south and the sun heats it up during the day. The surface temperature of the cliff face was significantly higher than the surrounding air temperature, and, on a hot summer day, this cliff face was almost unbearable. The overhang and tree also provided me with a tiny space to hide from the passing tour boats. Sometimes, I was more than happy to stop my work and wave every hour to the passing tourists. Other times, I was in the middle of working and I did not feel sociable. The small cave at this tree afforded me that luxury. Besides, my presence on the cliff face caused too much of a stir amongst the tourists. They would be pointing in my direction and the wavering voice on the boat intercom would be desperately fabricating a story that would explain why this man was clinging to the cliff face. I always wanted to do something bizarre like open a bright red umbrella or turn on a strobe light just to see how they might react. One day, I might just return to find out.

THE HUNCHBACK

> Location: Rattlesnake Point
> Basal Diameter: 16.1 centimetres
> Height (Living): 3.2 metres
> Cliff Height: 20.4 metres
> Date of Birth: 1411 A.D.
> Age in 2007: 597 years

Rattlesnake Point has been the most heavily climbed site in Ontario. It is (theoretically) the only cliff along the Niagara Escarpment where instructional climbing is allowed. It was also one of the first cliffs developed for climbing and it continues to attract heavy crowds, especially on weekends. Unfortunately, the cliff face is only 250 metres long. This intense climbing and hiking pressure has eliminated much of the native cliff plant community. There are also rumours that the defoliant Agent Orange was used to clear the talus vegetation in the late sixties!! The soil has long since eroded from around the roots of cliff-edge cedars. Ironically, casual visitors who have never seen undisturbed cliff edges often remark on this interesting root pattern, not realizing that the roots were once under a soil layer. Not surprisingly, I found that the density of cedars on the cliff face and along the cliff edge is significantly lower at Rattlesnake Point than at all other cliff sites in the region.

It came as a pleasant surprise therefore to find some old cedars at this site. Unfortunately, there are no middle-aged or young cedars on or near the cliffs, just old trees and rock. The levels of pedestrian and climbing traffic along this cliff are not conducive for the establishment and survival of young trees. Once the old cedars die, no younger generations will take their place. Eventually much of this cliff will be completely devoid of life.

RAT-579 was the oldest tree discovered at Rattlesnake Point and it grows in one of the few isolated clumps of vegetation hiding on the cliff face. I investigated this part of the cliff face directly because it was impossible to see from either the top or bottom of the cliff. I was actually focused on a completely different tree as I rappelled down the face, but next to it there grew a rather healthy looking cedar with lots of foliage. I could not see its base, so I lifted a few branches to investigate its architecture. There sat RAT-579, its base completely hidden by the branches of its neighbour, the branches of the two trees intermingled and indistinguishable from each other.

At just over three metres in length, it is hunched over like an old man. Rooted below its neighbour, it grows straight up into it, the hunchback marking the point where the trunks of the two trees meet. It then plunges back down the cliff face, its branches growing outwards towards the light. A thin stem-strip of living barked tissue supports the remaining foliage. Joan of Arc, Christopher Columbus, Montezuma, Michelangelo, Leonardo da Vinci, Johannes Gutenberg and Nicolaus Copernicus had not yet been born in 1411 when this tree began life on the cliff. Rattlesnakes actually lived at Rattlesnake Point.

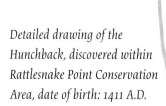

Detailed drawing of the Hunchback, discovered within Rattlesnake Point Conservation Area, date of birth: 1411 A.D.

Considering the high probability of past and future human intervention on these cliffs, let's hope that this tree can avoid detection for many years to come.

THE THREE KINGS

> Location: Lion's Head
> Basal Diameters: 69.4, 74.8 and 83.8 centimetres
> Heights (Living): 8.65, 10.50 and 7.80 metres
> Cliff Height: 20.4 metres
> Dates of Birth: 848 A.D., 971 A.D. and 1048 A.D.
> Ages in 2007: 1,160, 1,037 and 960 years

Of the Escarpment sites visited to date, the most spectacular and oldest cliff cedars are found on the cliffs within Lion's Head Provincial Nature Reserve. A walk in the talus is often rewarded with the discovery of ancient cedars, so ideally I'd like to spend my time scanning the cliff face above me. Unfortunately, the talus at Lion's Head is particularly unruly. It is often difficult to distinguish the rocks that are safe to step on from the ones that will rocket down the slope with you as its only passenger. My time is therefore split between craning my neck upwards at the cliff face and quick glances at my meandering feet and my next anticipated steps.

In August 2003, I came around a bend in the cliff face and adjusted my balance for a good look at the cliff face above. Finding nothing of interest, I readjusted my gaze towards my intended course. My eyes fell upon a cluster of four spectacular gnarled and ancient cedars. I gasped and vaulted across the rocks. Even though these cedars were rooted in the talus and not on the cliff face, I knew instantly that they could be older than 1,000 years. Careful examination of their trunks revealed that one cedar was dead, but the other three were very much alive. They resembled more streamlined versions of the bristlecone pines (the oldest trees on earth) that grow on rocky slopes at high altitudes in the White Mountains in California. Their name came naturally and without hesitation.

It's a mystery as to how these three trees have survived a continuous aerial bombardment of rocks peeling off the cliff face above, especially when they were younger and smaller than they are today. The talus is so loose here that it is difficult to believe that these cedars even got established at this spot! In later life, one cedar was even sliced open by razor-sharp slab of limestone. A piece of this rock snapped off and is still embedded in the wound.

Final ring counts place the ages of these cedars at 960, 1,037 and 1,160 years. These are the oldest white cedars on earth that are not rooted on a cliff face! For a thousand years, they have endured all that nature could throw at them. The surface of the dead wood is an intriguing complex of weathered cracks and bumps not unlike the weathered face of an old man. A closer look reveals that the bumps are a tight series of stumps marking points where branches have died or snapped off over the centuries. The dead wood begins at the down-slope side of the tree's base where the roots have been exposed by shifting rock. One cedar looks like it was tied into a knot, its direction of growth seemingly at whimsy. Another has a small garden of geraniums growing on its surface! All three lean towards Georgian Bay as though they're desperately trying to flee the dangers inherent in this spot. Unfortunately, trees usually have no choice but to remain in the place of their birth, and, while The Three Kings cannot really escape, I wonder how much longer they can eke out a living here. I wish I could come back in a few hundred years to find out.

The Three Kings, discovered within Lion's Head Provincial Nature Reserve; dates of birth, from top to bottom: 971 A.D., 1048 A.D. and 848 A.D.

The Snake, discovered within Lion's Head Provincial Nature Reserve: dates of birth, 795 A.D.

THE SNAKE

Location: Lion's Head
Basal Diameter: 22.0 centimetres
Height (Living): 4.5 metres
Cliff Height: 28.0 metres
Date of Birth: 795 A.D.
Age in 2007: 1,213 years

Trees don't float in mid-air. Of that, I am certain. Yet when I first got a clear look at this cedar, it didn't appear to be attached to the cliff face. It appeared as if someone had removed it from somewhere else, flipped it upside down and glued it to the rock. Only when I arrived at the tree's base did I find a very thin discrete horizontal crack less than five millimetres wide! The crack extended for at least twelve metres along the face but was almost invisible. The entire root

system of this cedar is therefore crammed into a space just a few millimetres wide but within a sprawling area of unknown extent stretching back and into the cliff face. Its root system is sandwiched
between two massive blocks of dolomite like a treasured leaf pressed
for safekeeping between the pages of a book.

For 1,213 years, this cedar has hung from this spot and survived;
extracting all the water and nutrients it needs for survival from this
confined space. It is hard to imagine that it has withstood centuries of
bombardment by all manner of natural disturbances including wind,
ice, snow, hail, rain and intense heat and cold. This cedar germinated
around the time of the first Viking raids in Britain and Ireland and
before the rule of the first Saxon kings. It was already over 700 years
old when Giovanni Caboto discovered the east coast of Canada!

The cedar itself looks like it has been extruded onto the cliff by
a giant cake decorator. Like icing, its stem oozes out of the crack and
snakes its way back and forth down the rock. Death of most of the
stem early in its life created unidirectional radial growth during the
following centuries. As a result, the stem is now flattened, but the
reasons for its meanderings back and forth across the rock are
unknown. From its base, the stem takes four sudden 180° turns in its
principal growth direction before the appearance of the first living
branch less than halfway down the length of the tree. It isn't possible
to reconstruct the events that led to these sudden directional
changes, but it has resulted in an elegant fluidity to the tree's shape.

THE ANCIENT ONE

> Location: Lion's Head
> Basal Diameter: 68.8 centimetres
> Height (Living): 6.9 metres
> Cliff Height: 19.0 metres
> Date of Birth: 688 A.D.
> Age in 2007: 1,320 years

It is the Koh-i-noor diamond of the Niagara Escarpment – a living
crown jewel. It may lack the polish of a precious stone, but it is an

The Ancient One,
discovered within
Lion's Head
Provincial Nature
Reserve: date of
birth, 688 A.D.

awe-inspiring sight. Tucked away on a ledge under a massive over-hang overlooking the waters of Georgian Bay, this cedar is the oldest living tree on the Niagara Escarpment, the oldest tree in Ontario and quite possibly the oldest living tree in Canada. When it began life, Mohammed, the founder of Islam, had been dead only 56 years. The Vikings had yet to colonize England and Leif Ericsson had yet to lose his way and find the North American coast. Gunpowder and playing cards had not been invented. There had been no Crusades, no Inca Kingdom in Peru, no Mongol hordes, no Ming Dynasty, no United States of America, no cars, no television, no Big Macs and no Britney Spears.

It is the oldest of the old. It contemplates life from a small ledge at the mouth of a cave, like an old sage perched on a mountain side. Its form reflects the polished shape of the cliff behind it. As this cedar grows, it follows the contours of the rock and mimics its form. Its massive base occupies the full width of the ledge. I could not access it without first landing in its crown and following this stem downwards through a sea of living and dead branches that tugged and ripped holes in my clothing. I arrived at the tree base, perched myself on the ledge and tried to figure out the best approach to obtaining a tree core.

I identified the original axis of the tree, the best place from which to obtain the core. Unfortunately, coring a cliff cedar is rarely a straightforward process. If you can work around the complex morphologies of the trees and the inconveniences of coring adjacent to rock then turbulent winds sometimes blow the core out of your hands. While these are predictable hazards, it sometimes best to expect the unexpected. This marked one such occasion.

On my first attempt at coring, the borer reached a point within the tree that offered no resistance, a sure sign that the tree was hollow. This isn't unusual as rot is often localized and concentrated at the cedar's base. As I steadied myself on the narrow ledge, I extracted the partial core and began a quick estimate of its age. There were hundreds of tree rings! Suddenly, and before I could finish, I felt a sharp but concentrated pain on the back of my right hand. Then another. I lurched back against the cliff face. A crowd of ants was scrambling over my arm and a column of ants was pouring out the end of the borer. From here, they were launching a successful military offensive against my exposed flesh. I removed the borer, sealed the hole to cut off the attack and with a small twig I flicked the offending militia off the cliff face and let them parachute into the talus below. My second (and first ant-free) attempt was much more successful. The tree was obviously close to a thousand years old. This core almost included the pith and it eventually allowed me to determine that it was approximately 1,320 years in age, the oldest living cedar and oldest living tree in Canada, east of British Columbia.

Despite the shock of attack, I felt somewhat assured and comforted that in its own way, the cedar fought against my attempts to determine its age. Centuries and generations of ants have probably lived here, and like a king's army behind castle walls they set upon me to protect their home. I can hardly begrudge them for that.

CHAPTER 10

LOOKING FORWARD

The Niagara Escarpment is the perfect escape. It is a ribbon of wilderness and rural beauty cutting across this huge heavily populated region. It is just a miracle, through a fluke of history and nature, that it remains today at all.[1]

Robert Bateman, 1989

Trees are held sacred by cultures around the world. Tribes in Fiji claim their descent from trees. Each tribe has a special tree that forms its tribal badge. In Shimonishimura, Japan, legend says that all those who use chopsticks made from one 900-year-old tree will never suffer from toothache and will live a long life. The peepal tree of India is considered the permanent seat of the gods and worshippers pour milk and water on its roots. It is also capable of blessing women with fertility. In central Africa, certain trees are thought to be inhabited by gods whose spirits will cause mass destruction if they are cut down. In Bavaria, some trees were thought to bring fertility to newlyweds who sat underneath them after midnight (no doubt!).

Unfortunately, trees are often seen as commodities or as obstacles to progress. The expansion of the human population across the planet, and the short-term economic gain garnered through clear-cutting and the conversion of land for agriculture has drastically reduced the surface area of the planet under forest cover. A recent study by Eric Anderson and colleagues at the Wildlife Conservation

A dusting of late autumn snow covers a cliff face near Meaford.

Society in New York revealed that 83% of the land surface of the earth (outside Antarctica) has been influenced by the human footprint, i.e. human densities greater than one person per square kilometre, agricultural land use, built-up areas or settlements, access to roads, major rivers or coastlines, or nighttime light bright enough to be detected by satellite sensor. Ecologist E.O. Wilson calculated four earths would be required to meet the resource needs of earth's population if everyone consumed at the level of the average U.S. inhabitant.

By 1920, 90% of the original forest cover in southern Ontario had been converted to non-forest uses (as detailed in a recent study by the Federation of Ontario Naturalists). While trees have reappeared on 13% of the land base since this time (through planting or natural regeneration), they are obviously no replacement for the original forest cover. Over the last eighty years, the original forests have continued to disappear and some of the remaining tracts have been over-managed or disturbed. We have reached a point in this part of the country where trees older than 120 years are increasingly rare. For every acre of land in southern Ontario that nourishes trees this old, there are another 1,428 acres that do not! Despite these bleak statistics, it is difficult to believe that old-growth forests are *still* subject to development pressures.

Luckily, most of the Niagara Escarpment cliffs escaped this disturbance. While some cliffs were blasted or converted into quarries, roads or ski hills, most of the Escarpment escaped the large-scale conversion of southern Ontario into agriculture and urban infrastructure. If the cliff-face cedars were cognizant, most would have "thought" themselves lucky. After all, those bipedal human organisms proliferating across the flatter landscapes couldn't possibly invade their vertical world. Or could they? In the years following the Second World War, humans started to appear on cliffs as European immigrants introduced rock climbing to the open rock faces along the Escarpment near Toronto. Trees hundreds of years old came in direct contact with humans for the first time.

Like everyone else at the time (the scientific community included), these pioneering climbers had no idea they were looking at the oldest forest in eastern North America. Vegetation, including

cedars, was cleared off the cliffs to make way for new climbing routes. In the last 20 years, the advent of indoor climbing gyms and advances in climbing equipment has made rock climbing more popular than ever. It has spread to many other areas along the Escarpment, and sport climbing, which uses fixed "bolts" drilled into the face, has opened climbing to an even larger audience. A study of popular climbing crags in the Milton area has shown that the density of young and old cedars is significantly reduced along climbing routes. Sawn stumps and branches are visual reminders that the climbers have not simply chosen rock with fewer trees.

Climbers have felt unfairly centred out and insist that any damage they have caused is minimal when compared with large-scale damage inflicted by urban sprawl and aggregate extraction. Unfortunately for the climbing community, the ancient cedar forest is only found on the cliff face, talus and immediate cliff edge of the Niagara Escarpment, precisely the same habitats they frequent for climbing. They argue that hikers cause similar damage along the Escarpment but don't draw the same criticism, yet hikers have no direct contact with the oldest trees. Climbers are the only ones who could come in direct contact with the oldest trees on the cliff face. Climbers also fail to recognize that they must first hike into cliffs before they climb, thus doubling their impact.

The solution is not easy. There is a large and growing climbing community in the region, and landowners and managers will need to recognize climbing as a legitimate recreational activity that will and should continue along the Niagara Escarpment. Climbers need to realize that some restrictions may be required to preserve the cliff-face forest in perpetuity. One of the main problems is that climbers have had free rein of the Escarpment cliffs for over fifty years. No one ever told them when or where they could or couldn't climb and it is extremely difficult to modify behaviour that has been entrenched for such a long period of time. The climbing community will need to continue to educate themselves about the Niagara Escarpment. It is more than just an outdoor climbing gym. It is a living ecosystem that is vulnerable to human impact and it represents part of the 17% of the earth's surface that has *not* been converted to human uses. If the climbing community can prove that they have made legitimate attempts to minimize impacts on the old-growth forest, then they will be helping themselves by ensuring continued access to their favourite crags. The persistence of this forest will depend on the cooperation and education of both landowners and the climbing community. The climbing community are stewards of this forest, whether they like it or not.

Why should climbers or anyone else for that matter care about old trees on the Niagara Escarpment? Why not open the earth's remaining wild areas (including the Niagara Escarpment) for general consumption or use. From a purely economic point of view, it doesn't make sense. A recent study in *Science* by Andrew Balmford and colleagues, looked at the costs of maintaining natural reserves on the planet compared with the benefits of converting that same habitat for short-term economic gain. They concluded that the benefit:cost ratio of an effective global conservation program at 100:1. A single year of habitat conversion on earth costs us collectively $250 billion this year and every year into the future. Imagine the complete elimination of the Niagara Escarpment due to private interests and short-term economic gain and it becomes easy to imagine the severity of those calculations.

Old-growth forests are also a vital and important part of our natural heritage. The more we expand our cities and build more urban infrastructure, the greater the demand will be for natural areas that have withstood this onslaught. They give us perspective for without them we have no way of gauging the severity of our actions on the natural world. And we like old trees. We may not know why, but we are attracted to them. Perhaps they provide comfort and reassurance to us that not everything has to change? We cling to them like an adult clings to the toys of their childhood. Perhaps we admire their tenacity in the face of adversity? For whatever reason, a majority of us would never begrudge this forest its right to exist, especially in light of what has already been lost.

The revelation that ancient trees still cling to the cliff faces of the Niagara Escarpment was of global significance because few places suddenly have more old-growth forest than they had before. We were given a second chance. The improbable became reality. But what will we do with this opportunity? In one hundred years time, how will we be judged on our treatment of this forest? Despite considerable media attraction to the Niagara Escarpment and the ancient cedars, the trees remain unprotected. We look at the way we treat this forest as a test of our species' capacity for altruism. If we can't recognize the importance of one thousand-year-old trees in the heart of an increasingly urbanized southern Ontario, what hope have we got for protecting anything else? We hope that you have gained respect and an aesthetic appreciation for trees that were hundreds of years old before Europeans set foot on this continent. Let us hope that they will still be there for others in the next millennium and beyond.

NOTES

PREFACE

1. From Sarah Anne Curzon, *Laura Secord, The Heroine of 1812: A Drama and Other Poems* (Toronto: C. Blackett Robinson, 1887).

CHAPTER 1: THE NIAGARA ESCARPMENT

1. William F. Moore, *Indian Place Names in Ontario* (Toronto: Macmillan, 1930) 36.

2. A glacial lobe is part of the glacial mass that moves like a bulge away from the main mass.

3. From *Cuesta*, official publication of the Niagara Escarpment Commission, Government of Ontario, Toronto, Spring 1979, 8.

4. Ibid, 7.

Chapter 2: Eastern White Cedar

1. Henry David Thoreau as quoted in A. Lounsberry and R. Ellis, *A Guide to Trees* (Toronto: W. Briggs, 1900) 104.

CHAPTER 3: THE GREAT MEDICINE TREE

1. Cyrus G. Pringle as quoted in M.L. Fernald and A.C. Kinsey, *Edible Wild Plants of Eastern North American* (New York: Harper and Row, 1943) 81.

2. R. Schlesinger and A.P. Stabler, *André Thevet's North America* (Kingston and Montreal: McGill-Queen's University Press, 1986) 8.

3.   Anthony J. Cichoke, *Secrets of the Native American Herbal Remedies* (New York: Avery, 2001) 125.

4.   Ibid.

5.   Charles F. Millspaugh, *American Medicinal Plants* (New York: Dover Publications Inc., 1974) 666. Reprint of an 1892 edition entitled Medicinal Plants. Philadelphia: J.C. Yorkston and Co.

6.   Ibid.

7.   Richard Hughes, *A Manuel of Pharmacodynamics* (London: London Press, 1876) 745.

8.   Henry D. Thoreau, as quoted in Fernald and Kinsey, *Edible Wild Plants of Eastern North America*, 81.

9.   Adapted from Alanson Skinner, "The Mascoutens or Prairie Potawatomi Indians, Part III, My Mythology and Folklore," in *Milwaukee Public Museum Bulletin,* 6 [3], 327-411.

10. Charles G. Leland, *The Algonquin Legends of New England* (Cambridge, MA: Houghton Mifflin and Co., Riverside Press, 1884) 96-98.

CHAPTER 4: CANOES, POSTS AND PILES

1.   Edward Allen Talbot, *Five Years Residence in Canada* (London: Longman, Hurst, Rees, Orme, Brown, and Green (2 Vols.), 1824) 283.

2.   Henry Y. Hind, *The Dominion of Canada: containing a historical sketch of the preliminaries and organization of confederation: also, the vast improvements made in agriculture, commerce and trade, modes of travel and transportation, mining, and educational interests, etc., etc. for the past eighty years under the provincial names: with a large amount of statistical information, from the best and latest authorities.* (Toronto: L. Stebbins, 1869) 131-133.

3.   Ibid.

4.   W.V. Kinietz, *The Indians of the Western Great Lakes 1615-1760* (Ann Arbor: University of Michigan Press, 1965) 41.

5.   Information regarding the lease between George Peavoy and Charles Connolly from Wellington Country Archives, Accession #A1952.286.3, Oct. 26, 1865.

6.   Phillip Henry Gosse, *The Canadian Naturalist* (London: J. Van Voorst, 1840) 12.

CHAPTER 5: THE FOREST OF THE ANCIENTS

1.   Doug Larson as quoted in *The Globe and Mail*, September 7, 1988, front page story.

2.   C.A. Faxon, *Faxon's Illustrated Handbook of Travel*. Boston, 1874. Quoted in Ralph Greenhill and Tom Mahoney, *Niagara* (Toronto: University of Toronto Press) 115. Original Faxon source not seen or available.

3.   G.M. Grant, *Picturesque Canada* (Toronto: Beldon Bros., 1882) 363.

4.   Hubert Ransier, "Hunting the hart's tongue and holly fern at Owen Sound, Ontario" in *American Fern Journal* Vol. 3, No. 2 (1913) 25-38.

5.   "Report on nature reserve candidates and other significant natural areas in the Niagara Escarpment Planning area." Parks Planning Branch, Division of Parks. Ontario Ministry of Natural Resources, 1976.

6.   Ibid.

7.   Taken from a proposal by George M. Stirrett and R.D. Muir, "Proposed national park – Report and appraisal from the biological and natural history viewpoint," 1963.

8. Joyce Gould, "A reconnaissance inventory of Mount Nemo Escarpment area, of natural and scientific interest," unpublished manuscript, 1985.

9. Ibid.

10. E. Schulman and W.R. Moore, "Bristlecone Pine, oldest living thing," in *National Geographic* Vol. 63 (1958) 355-372.

CHAPTER 6: NEXT STOP – THE WORLD!

1. Personal correspondence between Dr. Barthélèmy, Montpellier University, France, and Dr. D.W. Larson.

CHAPTER 7: THE ETERNAL OPTIMISTS

1. Andrew Douglass, "Dating Pueblo Bonito and Other Ruins in Southwest in *National Geographic*, Vol. 54, (1935) 737-770.

CHAPTER 8: THE HUNT FOR CANADA'S OLDEST TREES

1. Excerpt from Peter Kelly's field notes from June 24, 2003, describing the discovery of a 1,071-year-old cedar.

2. Quote is from Edmund Schulman, "Longevity Under Adversity in Conifers," in *Science*, Vol. 119 (1954), 396-399.

CHAPTER 9: CLOSE ENCOUNTERS

1. B. Stutz, "Stands of Time, in *Audubon*, Vol. 95, No. 1, (1993) 62-78.

CHAPTER 10: LOOKING FORWARD

1. Robert Bateman as quoted in Pat Keough and Rosemarie Keough, *The Niagara Escarpment – A Portfolio* (Don Mills, ON: Stoddart Publishing Co. Ltd., 1990) 11-12.

Selected Bibliography

Adolph, Val. *Tales of the Trees*. Delta, BC: Key Books, 2000.

Archambault, Sylvain and Yves Bergeron, 1992. "Discovery of a living 900-year-old northern white cedar, Thuja occidentalis, in northwestern Quebec" in *Canadian Field Naturalist*, No. 106, 1992, 192-195.

Arnold, Wilfred N. "Absinthe" in *Scientific American*, No. 260, 122-117.

Balmford, Andrew; Bruner, Aaron; Cooper, Philip; Costanza, Robert; Farber, Stephen; Green, Rhys E.; Jenkins, Martin; Jefferiss, Paul; Jessamy, Vaima; Madden, Joah; Munro, Kat; Myers, Norman; Naeem, Shahid; Paavola, Jouni; Rayment, Matthew; Rosendo, Sergio; Roughgarden, Joan; Trumper, Kate and R. Kerry Turner. "Economic reasons for conserving wild nature" in *Science*, 2002, No.297, 950-953.

Bartlett, Ruth M. and Douglas W. Larson, "The physiological basis for the contrasting distribution patterns of Acer saccharum and Thuja occidentalis at cliff edges" in *Journal of Ecology*, No. 78, 1990, 1063-1078.

_____, Uta Matthes-Sears and Douglas W. Larson, "Organization of the Niagara Escarpment cliff community. II. Characterization of the physical environment," in *Canadian Journal of Botany*, No. 68, 1990, 1931-1941.

_____, Uta Matthes-Sears and Douglas W. Larson, "Microsite-and age-specific processes controlling natural populations of Acer saccharum at cliff edges," in *Canadian Journal of Botany*, No. 69, 1991, 552-559.

_____, Richard J. Reader and Douglas W. Larson, "Multiple controls of cliff-edge distribution patterns of Thuja occidentalis and Acer saccharum at the stage of seedling recruitment," in *Journal of Ecology*, No. 79, 1991, 183-197.

Behr, E.A., "How durable is northern white cedar?" in *Michigan State University Extension Bulletin*, No. 929, 194, 5p.

Black, Meredith Jean, "Algonquin Ethnobotany: an interpretation of aboriginal adaptation in southwestern Quebec," in National Museum of Man Mercury Series, Canadian Ethnology Service Paper, No. 65, 1980.

Blasco, Steve M., (S. Parker and M. Munawar eds.) Geological history of Fathom Five National Marine Park over the past 15,000 years," in *Ecology, Culture and Conservation of a Protected Area: Fathom Five National Marine Park, Canada.* Leiden, The Netherlands: Backhuys Publishers, 2001, 45-62.

Blouin, Glen, *An Eclectic Guide to Trees East of the Rockies.* Erin, ON: The Boston Mills Press, 2001.

Booth, Barb and Douglas W. Larson, (E. Weiher and Paul Keddy eds.) "Impact of language, history, and choice of system on the study of assembly rules," in *Ecological Assembly Rules: Perspectives, Advances, Retreats. Edited by E. Weiher and Paul Keddy.* Cambridge, UK: Cambridge University Press, 1999, 206-229. "Constraints on the assembly of cliff communities at the seedling stage," in *Ecoscience*, No. 7, 336-344.

Briand, Chris H., Usher Posluszny, Douglas W. Larson and Uta Matthes-Sears, "Patterns of architectural variation in Thuja occidentalis L. (eastern white cedar) from upland and lowland sites," in *Botanical Gazette*, No. 152, 1991, 494-499.

Briand, Chris H., Usher Posluszny and Douglas W. Larson, "Comparative seed morphology of Thuja occidentalis (eastern white cedar) from upland and lowland sites," in *Canadian Journal of Botany*, No. 70, 1992, 434-438.

_____, "Influence of age and growth rate on radial anatomy of annual rings of Thuja occidentalis L. (eastern white cedar)," in *International Journal of Plant Sciences*, No. 154, 1993, 406-411.

Cartier, André, Henry Chan, Jean-Luc Malo, Line Pineau, K.S. Tae and Moira Chan-Yeung, "Occupational asthma caused by eastern white cedar (Thuja occidentalis) with demonstration that plicatic acid is present in this wood dust and is the causal agent," in *Journal of Allergy and Clinical Immunology*, No. 77, 1986, 639-645.

Cleland, Charles E., *Rites of Conquest: The History and Culture of Michigan's Native Americans*. Ann Arbor: The University of Michigan Press, 1992.

Curtis, James D., "Preliminary observations on northern white cedar in Maine," in *Ecology*, No. 27, 1946, 23-36.

Curzon, Sarah Anne, *Laura Secord, The Heroine of 1812: A Drama: And Other Poems*. Toronto: C. Blackett Robinson, 1887.

Erichsen-Brown, Charlotte, *Use of Plants for the Past 500 Years*. Aurora, ON: Breezy Creeks Press, 1887.

Fernald, Merritt Lyndon and Alfred Charles Kinsey, *Edible Wild Plants of Eastern North America*. New York: Harper and Row, 1943.

Fox, W. Sherwood, *The Bruce Beckons*. Toronto: University of Toronto Press, 1952.

Greenhill, Ralph and Thomas D. Mahoney, *Niagara*. Toronto: University of Toronto Press, 1969.

Sen Gupta, Sankar, *Sacred Trees Across Cultures and Nations*. Calcutta: Indian Publications, 1980.

Haig, April, Uta Matthes and Douglas W. Larson, "Effects of natural habitat fragmentation on the species richness, diversity, and composition of cliff vegetation," in *Canadian Journal of Botany*, No. 78, 2000, 786-797.

Hind, Henry Y., *The Dominion of Canada: containing a historical sketch of the preliminaries and organization of confederation: also, the vast improvements made in agriculture, commerce and trade, modes of travel and transportation, mining, and educational interests, etc., etc. for the past eighty years under the provincial names: with a large amount of statistical information, from the best and latest authorities*. Toronto: L. Stebbins, 1869.

Johnston, William F., "Thuja occidentalis L. northern white cedar," in *Silvics of North America*, Volume 1. *Conifers*. (Russell M. Burns and Barbara H. Honkala, tech. coords.) Agriculture Handbook 654, U.S. Department of Agriculture, Forest Service, Washington, DC, 1900.

Keough, Pat and Rosemarie, *The Niagara Escarpment: A Portfolio*. Don Mills, ON: Stoddart Pulishing Co. Limited, 1990.

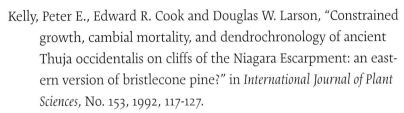

Kelly, Peter E., Edward R. Cook and Douglas W. Larson, "Constrained growth, cambial mortality, and dendrochronology of ancient Thuja occidentalis on cliffs of the Niagara Escarpment: an eastern version of bristlecone pine?" in *International Journal of Plant Sciences*, No. 153, 1992, 117-127.

_____, "A 1397-year tree-ring chronology of Thuja occidentalis from cliff faces of the Niagara Escarpment, southern Ontario, Canada," in *Canadian Journal of Forest Research*, No. 24, 1994, 1049-1057.

_____ and Douglas W. Larson, "Dendroecological analysis of the population dynamics of an old-growth forest on cliff-faces of the Niagara Escarpment, Canada," in *Journal of Ecology*, No. 85, 1997, 467-478.

"Effects of rock climbing on populations of presettlement eastern white cedar (Thuja occidentalis) on cliffs of the Niagara Escarpment, Canada," in *Conservation Biology*, No. 11, 1997, 1125-1132.

Kuhnlein, Harriet V. and Nancy J. Turner, *Traditional Plant Foods of Canadian Indigenous Peoples: Nutrition, Botany, and Use*. New York: Gordon and Breach Science Publishers, 1991.

Land Owner Resource Centre, "Extension Notes: Eastern White Cedar," Queen's Printer for Ontario, 1999.

Larson, Brendan M., John L. Riley, Elizabeth A. Snell and Helen G. Godscalk, *The Woodland Heritage of Southern Ontario*. Non Mills, ON: Federation of Ontario Naturalists, 1999.

Larson, Douglas W., "Effects of disturbance on old-growth Thuja occidentalis at cliff edges," in *Canadian Journal of Botany*, No. 68, 1990, 1147-1155.

_____, "Escarpment life: a whole different world," in *Bruce Trail News*, Fall, 1992, 20-23.

_____, Jen Doubt and Uta Matthes-Sears, "Radially sectored hydraulic pathways in the xylem of Thuja occidentalis as revealed by the use of dyes," in *International Journal of Plant Sciences*, No. 155, 1994, 569-582.

_____ and Peter E. Kelly, "The extent of old-growth Thuja occidentalis on cliffs of the Niagara Escarpment," in *Canadian Journal of Botany*, No. 69, 1991, 1628-1636.

_____, Uta Matthes-Sears and Peter E. Kelly, "Cambial dieback and partial shoot mortality in cliff-face Thuja occidentalis: evidence for sectored radial arcitecture," in *International Journal of Plant Sciences*, No. 154, 1993, 496-505.

_____, Uta Matthes-Sears and Peter E. Kelly, *Cliff Ecology; Pattern and Process in Cliff Ecosystems*. Cambridge, UK: Cambridge University Press, 2000.

_____, Uta Matthes, John A. Gerrath, Nick W. Larson, Jean M. Gerrath, Jeff C. Nekola, Gary L. Walker, Stefan Porembski and Alan Charlton, "Evidence for the widespread occurrence of ancient forests on cliffs," in *Journal of Biogeography*, No. 27, 2000, 319-331.

_____ and Lewis Melville, "Stability of wood anatomy of living and Holocene Thuja occidentalis L. derived from exposed and submerged portions of the Niagara Escarpment," in *Quaternary Research*, No. 45, 1996, 210-215.

_____, Steven H. Spring, Uta Matthes-Sears and Ruth M. Bartlett, "Organization of the Niagara Escarpment cliff community," in *Canadian Journal of Botany*, No. 67, 1989, 2731-2742.

Leland, Charles G., *The Algonquin Legends of New England, or, Myths and Folk Lore of the Micmac, Passamaquoddy, and Penobscot Tribes*. Cambridge, MA: Houghton, Mifflin and Co., Riverside Press, 1884.

Matthes-Sears, Uta and Douglas W. Larson, "Environmental controls of carbon uptake in two woody species with contrasting distributions at the edge of cliffs," in *Canadian Journal of Botany*, No. 68, 1990, 2371-2380.

_____ and Douglas W. Larson, "Rooting characteristics of trees in rock: a study of Thuja occidentalis on cliff faces," in *International Journal of Plant Sciences*, No. 156, 1995, 679-686.

_____ and Douglas W. Larson, "Limitations to seedling growth and survival by the quantity and quality of rooting space: implications for the establishment of Thuja occidentalis on cliff faces," in *International Journal of Plant Sciences*, No. 160, 1999, 122-128.

_____, Ceddy H. Nash and Douglas W. Larson, "Constrained growth of trees in a hostile environment: the role of water and nutrient availability for Thuja occidentalis on cliff faces," in *International Journal of Plant Sciences*, No. 156, 1995, 311-319.

_____, Christoph Neeser and Douglas W. Larson, "Mycorrhizal colonization and macronutrient status of cliff-edge Thuja occidentalis and Acer saccharum, in *Ecography*, No. 15, 1992, 262-266.

_____, Steve C. Stewart and Douglas W. Larson, "Sources of allozymic variation in Thuja occidentalis in southern Ontario, Canada," in *Silvae Genetica*, No. 40, 1991, 100-105.

Millspaugh, Charles F., *American Medicinal Plants*. New York: Dover Publications Inc., 1974.

Moss, Michael R. and W.G. Nickling, "Geomorphological and vegetation interaction and its relationship to slope stability on the Niagara Escarpment, Bruce Peninsula, Ontario," in *Géographie Physique et Quaternaire*, No. 24, 1980, 95-106.

Nelson, T.C., *A Reproduction Study of Northern White Cedar*. Lansing, MI:Game Division, Department of Conservation, Lansing, Michigan, 1951.

Niagara Escarpment Commission, "Public reaction to the preliminary proposals," in *Cuesta*, 1979.

Niagara Escarpment Commission, *The Niagara Escarpment Plan*. Toronto: Ministry of Environment and Energy, 1994.

Ontario Ministry of the Environment Pesticides Control Section, "Arborvitae Leaf Miners," Ontario Ministry of the Environment Facts about Pesticides, 6.

Sanderson, Eric W., Malanding, Jaiteh, Levy, Marc A., Redford, Kent H., Wannebo, Antoinette V., and Gillian Woolmer, "The human footprint and the last of the wild," in *BioScience*, No. 52, 2002, 891-904.

Seibel, George A., *Ontario's Niagara Parks*. Niagara Falls: The Niagara Parks Commission, 1985.

Stoltmann, Randy, *Guide to the Record Trees of British Columbia*. Vancouver: Western Canada Wilderness Committee, 1993.

Thwaites, Ruben G., *The Jesuit Relations and Allied Documents: travels and explorations of the Jesuit Missionaries in New France, 1610-1791: the orig-*

inal French, Latin, and Italian texts, with English translations and notes. Cleveland, OH: Burrows, Cleveland, 1897.

Tinkler, Keith J., "The Niagara Escarpment: physical features and human use.," in *Salzburger Geographische Arbeiten*, No. 28, 1995, 25-42.

Tovell, Walter M., *Guide to the Geology of the Niagara Escarpment.* The Niagara Escarpment Commission, 1992.

Ursic, Ken, Norm C. Kenkel and Douglas W. Larson, "Revegetation dynamics of cliff faces in abandoned limestone quarries," in *Journal of Applied Ecology*, No. 34, 1997, 289-303.

Van der Horst, A., "Surface morphological characteristics of talus slopes: Bruce Peninsula, Ontario," M.Sc. Thesis, unpublished, University of Guelph, Guelph, Ontario, 1985.

Van Pelt, Robert, *Forest Giants of the Pacific Coast.* Seattle, WA: Global Forest Society in Association with University of Washington Press, 2001.

Walker, Gary Lee., "Ecology and Population Biology of Thuja occidentalis L. in its Southern Disjunct Range," Ph.D. Dissertation, unpublished, University of Tennessee, Knoxville, Tennessee, 1987.

INDEX

ABOUT THE AUTHORS

PETER KELLY

Peter Kelly grew up in Lambeth, Ontario with a passion for the natural environment and photography. He received an Honours B.Sc and M.Sc. in Physical Geography from the University of Western Ontario. Here, he conducted fieldwork in the Canadian Cordillera and on Devon Island in the High Arctic. He has travelled extensively and photographed on all continents including Antarctica.

Peter joined the Cliff Ecology Research Group in 1989 for a summer inventory of ancient cliff-face forests along the Niagara Escarpment but just left the group after close to 17 years of ecological and conservation work on the ancient cedars of the Niagara Escarpment. He has co-authored two previous books related to cliff ecology; Cliff Ecology: Pattern and Process in Cliff Ecosystems (2000) and The Urban Cliff Revolution (2004). He has also published extensively in the popular and scientific press and given numerous talks to a broad range of audiences. Peter, along with Doug Larson, Uta Matthes and John Gerrath received a Niagara Escarpment Achievement Award from the Niagara Escarpment Commission in 2002 for their research efforts. He currently resides in Guelph, Ontario. www.peterkellyphotography.com

DOUGLAS LARSON

Doug Larson grew up in Oakville, Ontario and received his B.Sc. and PhD from McMaster University in Hamilton, Ontario. He joined the faculty of the Department of Botany at the University of Guelph shortly thereafter. Doug began his research on the coastal plains of the Canadian tundra but redirected his focus to the Niagara Escarpment in 1986 when he founded the Cliff Ecology Research Group.

Doug has won several teaching and research awards and has

published over 120 articles in the scientific press and is the senior author of two other books: *Cliff Ecology* and *The Urban Cliff Revolution.* He is currently a Professor in the Department of Integrative Biology and teaches both graduate and undergraduate students. He has also published numerous articles in the popular press and presented his findings at conferences and to smaller local audiences. He has shared the findings of the Cliff Ecology Research Group extensively with both broadcast and print media. He resides in Guelph, Ontario, with his wife Dawn. He spends his off-time building and playing guitars.